The Nostalgic Cook Book

Bill Habets

Copyright © MMIX The Windsor Group

Typeset by Raise Composition Ltd, London W1T 6PU

Published MMIX by The Windsor Group,
Hamilton House, 2 Station Road, Epping, Essex CM16 4HA

ISBN978-1-903904-80-0

Contents

Why and how yesteryear's recipes can help solve many of today's food-linked problems

Apart from the simple fact that it can be most interesting and edifying to delve into the recipes of the past as part of widening one's cookery skills and repertoire, there are yet more overwhelming reasons why engaging in that pursuit is more relevant than ever today, as the way to solve many of the food-related problems that affect all of us in these modern times can be found in how we cooked and what we ate in a bygone age.

Before looking at the solutions that recipes from the past can offer us, let's first examine the three major food-related issues that are troubling the nation as a whole at this time:

1. To begin with – and this is almost certainly the most important of the three – in recent years we have been experiencing what can only be described as an 'epidemic of obesity' that affects all age groups and which appears to be becoming steadily worse and worse. Key facts about obesity, as reported recently to Parliament by the National Audit Office, include:

   • A fifth of the adult population is now obese (21% of women and 17% of men). Additionally, most adults are either obese or overweight (32% of women and 46% of men are overweight). The picture is little better for children, as a recent survey found that 16%

of boys and girls aged 2 to 15 years are obese with a total of 30% being either overweight or obese. A third of young adults are either overweight or obese (32% of young men and 33% of young women). In addition, 9% of young men and 12% of young women are actually obese.

- Obesity is causing more than 30,000 premature deaths a year, a number that is rising steadily. It's estimated that everyone whose death is directly linked to obesity will have lost nine years of his or her life.

- Being overweight is a major cause of chronic and often incapacitating ill health, with heart disease, cancer, diabetes, high blood pressure and osteoarthritis all linked to the condition.

2. The cost of food has also been rising steadily in recent times, and it looks like that is a pattern that will be continuing for at least a few more years. While a cynical observer might comment that more expensive food means that people will be less likely to overeat, the equation is not quite that simple, as, in fact, the higher cost of wholesome and healthy foods often actually leads consumers, in an effort to balance their household budgets, to increasingly turn to cheaper but less nutritious alternatives, these all too often containing unhealthy amounts of saturated fats, salt and various additives.

3. Additionally, the form in which many modern foods are sold – including packs that provide bigger than actually required quantities, as well as unneeded packaging – is a cause of wastage at many levels: the consumers buy more than they require or can use, resulting in extra costs to them; getting rid of the uneaten food puts an extra burden on refuse collection and disposal; and, of course, this wasteful use of natural resources does not help the nation as a whole achieve a greener environment.

According to the experts, returning – or at least doing so to some appreciable degree – to a diet that broadly resembles the one that was enforced on the people of these islands because of food rationing during World War II and, to a lesser extent for the ten years that followed, would go a long way towards dealing with each and every one of these problems. Restricted though it may have been in many ways, the 'ration diet' did a great deal to improve the overall health of the nation. And if you think that the wartime diet, with all its restrictions, would compare poorly with the wide range of food choices we enjoy today, consider these facts:

- As far as controlling obesity is concerned, a recent comprehensive study that compared the weight and growth of schoolchildren fed on a 1950s diet with a similar group eating today's typical junk-food-rich menus found that modern children were consuming an average of 1,200 calories more than their counterparts of some 50 years ago, these extra calories making an obvious contribution to the obesity crisis.

- Despite the much lower calorie intake of children fed on the ration diet, they grew significantly taller than their modern opposites, while at the same time shedding considerably weight, so bringing their body mass indices broadly in line with what is considered healthy.

- Several independent research projects have come up with some startling facts when they compared the health of today's population with that of people who lived 50 to 60 years ago, finding that during the wartime and immediately post-war years, people were generally much healthier, hardly ever overweight, let alone obese if you exclude those individuals affected by certain specific disorders, and considerably less prone to heart disease, various forms of arthritic disease, diabetes (including the blindness that condition can cause), and even many types of cancer.

Summing it up, all recent research agrees that the vast majority of today's consumers would take a major step towards improving their health – and so substantially improving their chances of living considerably longer – if they were to revert to a diet similar to that of some 50 or more years ago.

A SHORT HISTORY OF RATIONING

To fully understand how the wartime diet – and its attendant health benefits – came into existence, it's useful to first briefly consider how food rationing worked, as this to a large extent explains why the population as a whole was so much healthier when the availability of most basic foodstuffs was either strictly controlled or simply not available.

Rationing was introduced on 8th January 1940, a time when the Government became acutely aware of two facts: first of all, it was clear that short of a German victory, the war was going to drag on for many years to come; and, secondly, even though vast amounts of food had been imported and stored before the outbreak of hostilities, that stockpile was only going to last a limited time. To make matters even worse, Britain was essentially under siege at the time as German submarines dominated the Atlantic, so bringing attempts by the merchant navy to ferry in further supplies from America nearly to a standstill.

Reluctantly, it was decided that the only way to avoid widespread food shortages in the future was to institute rationing. First to be rationed were imported foods like tea, coffee, sugar, chocolate, bacon, as well as all fruit from abroad, but these were soon followed by a much wider range of goods, including many non-food items, such as petrol, clothing and other textiles, and even soap. The way the system worked was that each person was given a ration book that contained a given number of coupons for each rationed food and these could be redeemed at a nationally preset price at the shop where the consumer had previously registered. Additional coupons were awarded to pregnant and nursing women, young children, and members of other special groups seen as having a greater need.

'Points' were also issued for tinned and imported foods and people were free to use their allocation as they wished – for example, six points enabled you to buy either a tin of sardines or two tins of fruit, provided, that is, that these items were actually available, which was by no means always the case.

As the war progressed, both what items were rationed and the amount of the weekly allowance for each changed frequently, in accordance with the current supply situation. Rationing of many basic foods continued for many years after the war and finally ended on 4th July 1954, nearly 15 years after its introduction.

To give you an idea of just how restrictive the rations were, and the extent to which they affected the average diet, this was the typical weekly ration for one person at the beginning of rationing and during the greater part of the war years:

- **MEAT:** approx. 6 ounces.

- **EGGS:** 1, later 2 eggs, and also supplemented by dried eggs.

- **FATS (BUTTER, MARGARINE AND LARD):** 4 ounces.

- **CHEESE:** 4 ounces.

- **BACON:** 4 ounces, initially only 2 ounces.

- **SUGAR:** initially 12 ounces, later reduced to 8 ounces.

- **TEA:** 2 ounces.

- **SWEETS:** 2 ounces.

Many foodstuffs, including bread, milk, vegetables, offal, chicken, rabbit and other game, and home-produced fruit, were never rationed, although these items were often in short supply or even unobtainable for brief periods.

It's obvious that having to cope within these meagre allowances needed a major shift in the average diet as well in the thinking of those who bought and prepared food, who at the time were mainly housewives. To achieve this, the Ministry of Food initiated a long-running national campaign throughout the war years and for some time thereafter aimed at achieving two goals: first, to encourage 'wise' cooking by creating recipes and promoting all sorts of dishes that could be concocted within the limitations of the rationing system; and, secondly, to ensure that no food was ever wasted. As a result of this ongoing campaign, many of the recipes in this book first saw the light of day, including the (in-)famous Lord Woolton Pie, the cakes and sweets that required no sugar, and the many and varied ways in which a tasty main meal could be fashioned from a humble herring. There were also some very unusual recipes, such as those for whale meat or snoek, a weird-looking South African fish, but these you will not find within these pages, on the relatively safe assumption that even if the raw product were obtainable today it would hold little appeal for most of us.

However, unlike whale and snoek, most of the recipes inspired by rationing remain remarkably appetising and enticing, even if judged by today's more demanding tastes. And, as has already been explained, these dishes from a past era, when forming a major and regular part of someone's food intake, will go a long way towards ensuring overall better health and greater longevity.

However, there are two more aspects of the wartime diet that were also found to have had a major impact upon just how nutritious and healthy it was, as we'll now discover...

RICH IN HEALTH-GIVING HERBS AND SPICES

The first of the factors likely to have made a substantial contribution to the health-giving aspects of yesteryear's meals is that, in order to offset the inherent lack of taste of dishes that contained no meat or fish or only relatively small amounts of either of these, most of the Ministry of Food recipes used quite generous helpings of many different herbs and spices. Many of these, apart from imparting all-important flavour, also provided some very notable and specific health benefits, as you'll see from the list that follows and which is based on the very latest nutritional research:

- **BAY LEAVES:** a rich source of essential oils, glycosides and bitter principles, these leaves, usually used dry in cooking, improve both the appetite and digestion.

- **CHIVES:** the slender, hollow leaves of this plant are a good source of vitamin C, vitamin B2, and carotene. Additionally, they contain significant amounts of sodium, calcium, potassium and iron, and are credited with helping reduce blood pressure, stimulate the digestive system and revive a flagging appetite.

- **CINNAMON:** the spice obtained from this tree – whether derived from its bark, leaves, twigs or roots – contains eugenol and cinnamol, an aldehyde. It was first recognised as a valuable general tonic in ancient Egypt.

- **CLOVES:** the dried unopened flower buds of this evergreen tropical tree, used as a pungent and fragrant spice, improves appetite and regulates digestion.

- **GINGER:** the underground stem of this plant, either used fresh or powdered as a flavouring, is a useful aid for stomach upset, and, as such, it is commonly recommended by healthcare professionals to help prevent or treat nausea and vomiting associated with motion sickness, pregnancy, and cancer chemotherapy.

- **ONION, COMMON:** the bulb of this humble plant contains a wide range of biologically valuable substances that stimulate the liver and pancreas, and even ease a frayed nervous system as well as help you ward off a cold.

- **PARSLEY:** the curled aromatic leaves of this garden plant are rich in vitamin C. Eaten in modest quantities, parsley aids digestion and also increases urinary output. **Pregnant women and people affected by kidney problems should avoid eating too much of it.**

- **PEPPER, BLACK:** although the amounts involved are usually fairly minuscule because of the quantity of pepper used in even the hottest of dishes, this condiment contains an alkaloid that irritates mucous membranes and so can promote digestion. It has also been shown to slightly stimulate heart activity.

- **ROSEMARY:** the evergreen leaves of this aromatic European shrub have been proven to stimulate the flow of both bile and gastric juices, thereby improving digestion. Additionally, rosemary can reduce smooth muscle spasm and reduce bacterial growth. **Note that this flavouring should be totally avoided in pregnancy, even as a seasoning.**

- **SAGE:** the leaves of this perennial Mediterranean plant contain several essential oils and more than ten per cent of tannin, as well as hormones and bitter principles, and have been found to aid digestion, restrict bacterial growth and reduce inflammation.

- **THYME:** this seasoning has a wide range of medicinal properties, having deodorant and disinfectant properties as well as being helpful in reducing stomach inflammation, flatulence and diarrhoea. **Note that expectant mothers and people with heart problems should avoid large amounts of thyme.**

- **VANILLA:** although not fully confirmed by modern research, vanilla is recognised by traditional medicine for eliminating tiredness and strengthening the heart.

- **WATERCRESS:** when used in cooking, the stalks and leaves of this perennial plant yield high percentages of vitamins C, A and E, and stimulate the activity of bile and so aid digestion. **Note that an excessive amount of watercress can irritate the urinary tract.**

These herbs and spices are readily available and it would make good sense for anyone planning to cook the 'old-fashioned way' to keep a stock of most of these in their larder.

BUYING SEASONAL PRODUCE AT ITS BEST

The second contributory factor that helped make Britain's wartime diet the healthiest ever enjoyed by any nation, is that just about all vegetables and fruit were fresh. In any recipe, and this applies particularly to most of those listed in this book, just how nutritious it will be is affected not only by its ingredients, but also by the quality of those ingredients.

In general, the nutritional values of all fresh produce will be at its highest when a given fruit or vegetable is in season, as it will not have deteriorated because of lengthy storage. And, because it's obvious that the health-giving properties of produce are not going to be enhanced by it having travelled perhaps thousands of miles before ending up on your supermarket shelf, it's also clearly best to always buy British produce whenever possible, so minimising the length of time between harvest and consumption.

To help you in your search for the freshest fruit and vegetables, there is an alphabetical list on page 14 (TABLE 1) of when British produce is normally in season. Note, however, that there will be local variations in the months indicated – the season usually being later in the year and shorter the further North you are – and that, being weather dependent, all produce can be affected by unusual meteorological conditions.

HOW TO MAKE THE WARTIME DIET WORK FOR YOU AND YOUR FAMILY

If, after reading the above, you're now keen on getting all the health and other benefits that can be obtained from the wartime diet for you and your family, here are some thoughts and suggestions that will help you introduce it successfully into your daily routine:

- To begin with, it's important to be aware that powerful though the wartime diet can be, it's not going to get very far delivering its benefits if you only now and then prepare a 'nostalgic' recipe. Though a particular wartime

TABLE 1	JAN	FEB	MAR	APR	MAY	JUN	JUL	AUG	SEP	OCT	NOV	DEC
Apples									■	■	■	
Asparagus					■	■						
Blackberries								■	■	■		
Blackcurrants						■	■	■				
Broad Beans						■	■					
Broccoli						■						■
Brussels Sprouts	■	■							■	■	■	■
Cabbage	■	■	■	■								
Calabrese						■	■					
Carrots	■	■										
Cauliflower						■	■					
Celery							■	■	■			
Cherries						■	■					
Courgette						■	■	■	■	■		
French Beans							■	■				
Gooseberries						■	■					
Kent Cobnuts									■			
Leeks	■	■	■	■				■	■	■	■	■
Mangetout						■	■	■	■	■		
Marrow								■	■			
Onions	■											
Parsnips	■	■							■	■	■	■
Pears									■	■		
Peas						■	■					
Plums								■	■			
Potatoes					■	■	■	■	■	■	■	
Pumpkins									■	■	■	
Purple Sprouting		■	■									
Raspberries						■	■	■	■			
Rhubarb				■	■							
Runner Beans							■	■	■			
Spinach						■	■	■		■		
Squash								■	■	■	■	
Strawberries						■	■					
Swede		■	■						■	■	■	■
Sweetcorn								■	■			
Tomatoes							■	■				
Turnips	■	■							■	■	■	■
Watercress			■	■	■							■

meal may be packed generously with a given set of nutrients that are good for you, its consumption is only really going to make a worthwhile difference if it is consumed as part of a general approach to food intake that broadly follows the wartime diet: less meat, a lot less sugar and fats, lots and lots of vegetables that are as fresh as possible, and smaller portions in general, and no unhealthy snacking between main meals!

- It follows from this that it is also not possible to single out particular recipes for specific health-giving properties. In other words, no matter how large the quantity of ingredients, beneficial, say, for reducing the risk of heart disease may be in a given recipe, you'll only reduce that risk by following an overall diet that's generally suited to that purpose. Accordingly, it's impossible – and could even be misleading – to recommend a recipe, or a group of them, as a means to improve specific health problems (although it can be argued that the no-sugar cakes in the recipes section can, of course, be particularly helpful to those seeking to lose weight). What will make the wartime diet work for you and yours will be the totality and variety of your food intake over a period of time. When the Ministry of Food experts first designed the ration system, they made sure that all nutritional requirements could be fully met within it, and when they created their recipes, they based them on what ingredients were going to be available. It is the combination of these two elements – the limited availability of certain foods that in turn led to dishes that relied as much as possible on fresh produce – that produced the long-term benefits.

- Naturally, eager though you may be to reap the health rewards of the wartime diet, it's not likely that you're going to want to rush into it headlong from the start. In fact, such a precipitous approach could all too easily turn out to be self-defeating, because tasty though the wartime recipes may be, it can take a while to get used to them, let alone the somewhat smaller portions that are part of the overall diet. A much better approach is to introduce the 'nostalgic' recipes gradually, starting off with perhaps two, maybe three, main meals a week, then after a while increasing the frequency with which they appear on the dinner table, until you reach the stage where all of your food intake is based on the wartime diet.

- To get other members of your family, who may less keen than you are on the wartime diet, to accept its gradual introduction, it can be a useful ploy to at times make minor adjustments to the recipes that follow, possibly increasing the meat and sugar content of some of them to make them more acceptable to today's taste buds that often require over-stimulation.

- Patience is a virtue that is never more tested than when you're eagerly awaiting the rewards that a change in eating habits is due to bring. While it's impossible to forecast just how quickly you may begin to experience the overall benefits of at least partially following the wartime diet, it's likely that once you've reached the stage where half or more of your main meals are based on it, you will start experiencing slow but steady weight loss, if that was your aim in the first place. Note, however, that the rate of weight loss, if any, will gradually reduce and stop altogether as you begin to reach your optimum weight. Other health benefits – such as reduced risks of heart disease, arthritic disorders, diabetes and cancer – are much more difficult to quantify, but it's fairly safe to say that these should start coming into effect within six months, or even less, of starting the wartime diet.

Of course, there is an all-important difference between how you will be experiencing the wartime diet and how it affected the people of Britain all those years ago: they had little choice in the matter, their choice of food was forced upon them by the restriction of the rationing system; you, on the other hand, can to a large extent experiment and modify the diet to match your personal requirements while at the same time ensuring that it still remains effective enough to provide the particular benefits you want it to deliver.

To help you devise your own personalised version of the wartime diet, there now follows some general guidelines about the latest thinking regarding healthy eating.

AN OPTIMUM DIET FOR OVERALL GOOD HEALTH

The idea that the cause as well as the cure for many, perhaps even most, of the illnesses and ailments that besiege us is to be found in what we eat is not exactly new, as exemplified by the proverb, believed to date back to the seventeenth century, that states: "Diet cures more than the lancet". There are many other famous time-honoured quotations that bear witness to the same belief, that the food we consume determines just how healthy – or unhealthy – we are, including:

- "Let thy food be thy medicine and thy medicine be thy food." HIPPOCRATES (460-377 B.C.)

- "The Chinese do not draw any distinction between food and medicine." LIN YUTANG (1895-1976), writing in *The Importance of Living.*

And, of course, there is the oft-quoted proverb whose origins are lost in the mists of time that promises, "An apple a day keeps the doctor away".

What all of these sayings have in common is to proclaim the simple fact that any person's state of health is to a large extent a direct result of the food he or she consumes.

This naturally raises the question: what foods should we eat, and in what quantities, to provide ourselves with a diet that can be called 'optimum' in that it provides everything we need to enjoy robust good health for as many years as possible.

Although the exact answer to that question would depend to a large extent upon the individual concerned, there are some generally accepted guidelines that apply to all of us.

To begin with, the experts all agree that a good overall diet is one that provides several vital components in the right proportions on a regular basis, the main ones of these being:

- Calories for energy.

- Proteins, fats, and carbohydrates.

- Vitamins.

- Minerals and trace elements.

- Water.

- Roughage.

Although it is comparatively simple to determine what components a diet needs to provide, it is much more difficult to quantify these. For example, there can be a tremendous variation in the individual need for calories. Equally, there can be considerable individual differences in the need for other nutrients. Naturally, to prevent obesity, it's vital that the intake of energy-producing foods more or less matches that of energy needed over a period of time – if the average food intake is too great, some of it will be converted into fat, so leading to obesity and all of its attendant risks; if the food intake isn't adequate, then there may be tiredness, lassitude, and lethargy, and the body may even start to consume its own fat to meet the need, a process that in the extreme leads to starvation. This means that a delicate balance always needs to be maintained by eating just enough energy-producing foods to provide all that's necessary, but no more than that.

While there are many complicated and highly-sophisticated methods for working out individual calorie requirements – which can vary greatly, according to age, gender, the amount of physical energy expended, as well, as in the case of women, whether they are pregnant or breastfeeding – it all too soon becomes only too obvious whether you're overeating or not, because if you are you will gradually but steadily keep piling on the pounds and your amount of body fat will increase, until it becomes quite evident that you're overweight.

As you'll already have guessed, all the factors mentioned allow for many, many permutations and it is therefore almost impossible to state categorically just how much energy-producing food people should eat as the number of variables are just too many.

And if such a calculation is difficult enough for something as relatively simple as energy requirements, it becomes truly impracticable when looking at all the components of an average diet. Certainly, the scientists have worked out what they call 'Estimated Average Requirements' – known as EARs – for most nutritional components, but they frankly admit that these are indeed estimates and not hard and fast recommendations.

And if calculating dietary requirements were not already enough of a problem, this becomes even more complicated when you try to relate that information to specific food or nutrient intakes. There are three main reasons for this:

- One very basic one is that there is no accepted definition of 'optimal health', and therefore how can one assert that to obtain this desirable, but ill-defined state you need X amount of nutrient A and Y of food B?

- There are extremely wide variations in how much of the nutrients contained in food are actually absorbed by the body. For example, only about 15 per cent of the iron contained in foods consumed does in fact get into the body on the average, but the absorption rate of this mineral can drop to as little as half as much for many people. There are equally large possible variations in absorption rates of many other nutrients.

- Although it is comparatively easy to determine how much of a given nutrient is needed to avoid deficiency-linked symptoms for most people – such as what is the smallest amount of vitamin C that will prevent scurvy – it is a totally different matter to decide whether larger amounts would provide additional benefits to contribute to the 'optimal health' ideal.

As Recommended Daily Allowances (RDAs) are now almost universally acknowledged as failing to provide a full answer to what's a good diet, nutritionists have instead come up with a much better way of providing guidance about what you should eat. This new way of thinking is incorporated in *The National Food Guide – The Balance of Good Health*, published by the Health Education Authority. Although this guide more or less forgets RDAs and complicated calculations involving these, it instead presents straightforward guidance on how to achieve a balanced diet. To keep things simple, the guide concentrates on five key food groups and suggests what your intake of each of these should be.

The five food groups are:

1) Bread, other cereals (including pasta, rice, and also beans and pulses) and potatoes. The basic guidance offered is that one should 'eat lots' of these because they are good sources of carbohydrates (as starch), fibre, and also contain B complex vitamins as well as a certain amount of iron and calcium. Additionally, it's recommended that these foods should not be eaten too often in a fried form or have too much fat added to them.

2) Fruits and vegetables, not only fresh, but also in juice, tinned, or dried forms. As these are good low-calorie sources of vitamin C, carotenes, folates as well as providing fibre and some carbohydrates, the guide once again recommends that you should 'eat lots' of these, but with as little sugary or fatty sauces or dressings as possible.

3) Milk and dairy foods, these including cheese, yoghurt and fromage frais, but excluding cream, butter, and eggs. Although these foods are excellent sources of vitamins A, D, and B12, as well as of calcium and protein, they do however often also have a high fat content. Because of that

dual aspect, the guide recommends you should 'eat or drink moderate amounts' of these foods, opting for a lower fat version whenever possible.

4) Meat and fish, but also included in this group are poultry, eggs, nuts, and – once again – beans and pulses. While some of these foods can also be high in fat, they are otherwise good sources of protein, iron, various B complex vitamins, zinc, and magnesium, so the overall recommendation is that you only eat a moderate amount of these, choosing those with the lowest fat content.

5) Fatty and sugary foods, including butter, margarine, spreading fats, cream, chocolate, cooking oils, as well as processed or packaged foods with a high content of any of these ingredients. Although these foods do provide some vitamins and essential fatty acids, they also contain a great deal of fat, sugar, and salt. Accordingly, the guide suggests that you should consume these sparingly.

Some other main recommendations from the guide:

• That a variety of foods from the first four groups should be eaten every day to provide the range of nutrients needed to keep the body healthy and functioning properly. Additionally, you should increase your range of nutrients even further by not always choosing the same foods from each group, but varying these as much as possible.

• Most people would benefit from eating more fruit and vegetables than they do currently. The guide suggests that you should aim at having five or even more portions of these every day.

• The guide also suggests that most people would also benefit from increasing their intake of bread, other cereals, and potatoes.

- It also stressed that everyone should drink plenty of fluid, six or eight cups or glasses of it daily, but keep the intake of sugar-laden drinks to a minimum.

What is truly interesting about the many recommendations above, which encapsulate the latest 'modern' thinking about what constitutes a generally healthy diet for most people, is that they so closely match the diet that was enforced on the population of these islands during the war and immediate post-war years, either because of rationing or shortages. So it seems that by going back to some old-fashioned ideas of what to eat, we're in fact following the dictates of the most up-to-date scientific advice about food intake!

The Nostalgic Cook Book Recipes

To help you get the most from the recipes that follow, here are a few explanatory notes about some of the ingredients and terms you'll frequently encounter in them and with which today's cooks may not be all that familiar.

DRIED EGGS

Fresh eggs were severely rationed in World War II, initially restricted to one egg per person a week, this later increasing to two eggs. However, this meagre ration was to be supplemented to some extent in May 1941 when dried egg powder was first imported from America. Initially, each family was allowed one packet – which could be reconstituted to produce the equivalent of 12 eggs – every eight weeks, but this was later increased to a packet every four weeks.

Here is what the Government had to say about dried eggs:

"The Ministry of Food dried egg is pure fresh egg with no additions, and nothing but the moisture taken away. It is pure egg, spray-dried. Dried eggs are just as good as fresh eggs, and should be used in the same way. However, for some recipes dried eggs should be reconstituted", and then went on to explain the three different ways this could be done:

1. Mix the egg and water and allow to stand for about five minutes until the powder has absorbed the moisture.

Then work out any lumps with a wooden spoon, finally beating with a fork or whisk.

2.   Mix the egg to a smooth paste with half the water. Beat till lumps have been removed. Add the remaining water and beat again.

3.   For plain cakes and puddings, batters, etc., the egg can be added dry and mixed with the other dry ingredients. When adding the liquid to the mixture an additional 2 tablespoons per dried egg used must be allowed.

Once reconstituted, the egg should be used immediately, the Ministry advised further, and should be used in recipes exactly as fresh eggs, beating as usual before adding to other ingredients.

Today's cooks may have some difficulty in buying dried eggs, although they are generally available from camping suppliers as well as some supermarkets. When one of the following recipes calls for 'dried' or 'reconstituted' eggs, follow these guidelines:

- If the ingredient is specified as 'reconstituted' dried eggs, just use fresh eggs instead.

- If the recipe specifies that dried eggs should be used, you can usually still use fresh eggs, but reduce the amount of any liquid added to the mix by about two tablespoons for each egg.

NOTE: Household milk in recipes is powdered milk. To make up, follow instructions on packaging.

THE 'NATIONAL' LOAF

You'll also find the occasional reference to 'national bread' – this was bread made with more grain than white bread and produced a brown loaf. Today's nearest equivalent is wholewheat bread, which can be safely substituted for national bread. In most recipes ordinary white bread will also serve just as well. Also, the nearest equivalent to 'national flour' is wholewheat flour.

OVEN TEMPERATURES

The modern cook, used to having oven temperatures expressed as being 'x' degrees, may also find the various mentions of a 'moderate' or 'cool' oven a bit confusing. Here, to get you on the right track, is a conversion table of what those rather vague expressions really mean:

OVEN TEMPERATURE	DEGREES FAHRENHEIT	GAS REGULO	DEGREES CELSIUS
Cool oven	225-250	0-½	107-121
Very slow oven	250-275	½-1	121-125
Slow oven	275-300	1-2	135-149
Very moderate oven	300-350	2-3	149-177
Moderate oven	375	4	190
Moderately hot oven	400	5	204
Hot oven	425-450	6-7	218-233
Very hot oven	475-500	7-9	246-260

Be aware that this table can only serve as an approximate guide as ovens vary greatly and their thermostats are often less than wholly accurate. Accordingly, you may have to make some allowance for the peculiarities of your oven, either by setting its dial higher or lower than suggested or by altering cooking times slightly.

SPOONS

Finally, please note the following points about the various weights and measures mentioned in this section:

- Weights and measures are British (similar terms are used in America, but some of them are defined differently there).

- When quantities are expressed as different types of 'spoons', these always indicate a level spoonful.

- A British standard tablespoon equals 1 fluid ounce.

- Three 'teaspoons' equal one 'tablespoon', or ⅓ of a fluid ounce.

Finally, please note that unless otherwise indicated, the recipes that follow are meant to serve four persons ... or to quote the Ministry of Food, "sufficient for four", which is not quite the same thing, depending upon your appetite.

Breakfast Recipes

Just like today's dieticians, the Ministry of Food experts during the wartime years were acutely aware that a good breakfast was the essential foundation upon which a health-giving diet was built.

Accordingly, they produced a series of recommendations that are every single bit as valid today as they were then.

Reminding everyone that "a good breakfast every day is the first rule in the book of health", they came up with these...

SUGGESTIONS FOR BREAKFAST

Get up early enough to enjoy breakfast without hurry. A cup of tea and a morsel of toast gulped down with one eye on the clock is no use to anyone. Breakfast is an important meal for all of us, but especially important for growing school children and young factory workers.

BREAKFAST MENU

PORRIDGE
(or other cereal with fruit or milk)

COOKED DISH
(Bacon or fish or meat or cheese or egg with fried potatoes or fried bread)

NATIONAL or WHOLEWHEAT BREAD
with
BUTTER or MARGARINE
and
MARMALADE or JAM or other SWEET SPREAD

TEA or COFFEE
COCOA or MILK for children

While this suggested breakfast menu may seem like altogether too much for many of us nowadays, it's worth keeping the following points in mind:

- Numerous studies have shown that people who want to lose weight will generally stand a better chance of achieving their goal if they eat quite a hearty breakfast. The reason for this is simple: having a substantial breakfast keeps the 'munchies' at bay and so reduces the temptation to fill up during the day by frequent snacking on foods that usually have a high sugar content.

- Other studies have confirmed that starting the day with a decent breakfast can substantially increase the ability to work and think, enabling us to cope better with the stresses of the day.

SCRAMBLED EGG (ONE PORTION)

1 dried egg (reconstituted or fresh)   *1 tablespoon milk*
½ oz. fat   *Salt and pepper*

METHOD

Add the milk and seasoning to the egg and beat lightly with a fork. Melt the fat in a saucepan, add the mixture and cook over a very low heat, stirring as little as possible until it just sets. Serve at once.

NOTE: To make this dish go further, diced cooked vegetables can be added.

MOCK FRIED EGG (ONE PORTION)

1 dried egg (reconstituted)   *Salt and pepper*
2 slices wholewheat bread

METHOD

Beat the egg. Cut holes from the centre of each slice of bread with a small scone cutter. Dip the slices quickly in water and then fry on one side until golden brown. Turn on to the other side, pour half the egg into the hole in each slice of bread, cook till the bread is brown on the underneath side, The bread cut from the centres can be fried and served with the slices.

TOMATO CHEESE SAVOURY

4 tomatoes or 1 lb. cooked   *3 oz. grated cheese*
*   mixed vegetables*   *Salt and pepper*
1 lb. mashed potatoes

METHOD

Cut tomatoes into slices or dice the cooked vegetables and place on a bed of mashed potatoes. Sprinkle with grated cheese, salt and pepper. Put under the grill until cheese has melted and browned. Serve hot.

OATMEAL CHEESE RAREBIT (ONE PORTION)

1 oz. grated cheese   *¼ pint water*
1 oz. toasted oatmeal   *Salt and pepper*
1 oz. flour   *1 teaspoon coarsely chopped parsley*
1-1½ lb. mashed potatoes

METHOD

Mix flour with enough water to make a smooth paste. Boil the remaining water and add the flour paste, boiling for one minute. Add the cheese, oatmeal and seasoning, stir well and cook for a minute or two longer. Pour on to a flat bed of mashed potato and place under grill until brown. Sprinkle with parsley before serving.

PORRIDGE (I)

4-6 oz. oatmeal　　　　　*1 teaspoon salt*
2 pints water

METHOD

Soak the oatmeal in the water overnight. Next morning, add salt, bring to the boil and cook for 15-20 minutes, stirring occasionally to prevent sticking.

NOTE: If thick porridge is preferred, use the larger amount of oatmeal.

PORRIDGE (II)

6-8 oz. rolled oats　　　　*1 teaspoon salt*
*　or barley flakes*　　　　*2 pints water*

METHOD

Mix the rolled oats or barley flakes with a little of the cold water. Boil the rest and pour on to the oats or flakes stirring well. Return to the pan. Add the salt and boil the porridge for 5-10 minutes, stirring at intervals.

NOTE: If thick porridge is preferred, use the larger amounts of rolled oats or barley flakes.

SEMOLINA PORRIDGE

4-6 oz. semolina　　　　*2 pints liquid (1 pint or less milk*
1 teaspoon salt　　　　　*and remainder in water)*

METHOD

Blend the semolina and salt with a little of the cold liquid. Bring the remainder to the boil and pour on to the blended semolina. Return to the pan and boil gently for 15-20 minutes, stirring well to prevent it burning.

NOTE: If thick porridge is preferred, use the larger amount of semolina.

WHEATMEALIES

Cut bread into small dice not more than ½" thick. Spread on a flat tin and bake until quite crisp. Serve with milk and sugar or with stewed fruit.

SUMMER BREAKFAST DISH

4 oz. rolled oats or barley flakes   *½-¾ grated apple*
   or kernels   *1-2 tablespoons sugar*
4 tablespoons milk

METHOD

Soak the rolled oats or barley flakes or kernels overnight in barely enough water to cover. In the morning, beat up well with the other ingredients. This is a delicious alternative to porridge on summer mornings.

FRIED BREAD AND BACON

4 rashers bacon   *4 slices bread ¼" thick*
Fat for frying, if necessary   *(from a 1 lb. loaf)*

METHOD

Fry the bacon and push to one side or remove from the pan and keep hot. If the bacon is lean it may be necessary to add a little extra fat to have enough to cover the bottom of the pan. Fry the slices of bread in the hot fat until golden brown on both sides. Serve with the bacon.

BACON TURNOVERS

1-2 rashers fat bacon
4 oz. plain flour with
   2 teaspoons baking powder
   or 4 oz. self-raising flour

½ teaspoon salt
½-1 teaspoon mixed herbs
4-6 tablespoons milk

METHOD

Fry and chop the bacon, keeping the fat to fry the turnover. Mix the dry ingredients to a scone dough with milk and roll to ¼" thickness. Cut into eight 3" rounds and place bacon in the centre of four. Dampen edges and cover with remaining four rounds. Fry in the bacon fat for about 10 minutes until cooked through and golden brown on both sides.

FRITTERS

4 oz. self-raising flour
   or 4 oz. plain flour and
   2 teaspoons baking powder
2 oz. chopped bacon

1 teaspoon salt
¼ teaspoon pepper
¼ pint milk (approx.)
Fat for frying

METHOD

Mix flour, baking powder, if used, salt and pepper well together. Mix to a stiff batter with the milk. Beat well. Add the chopped bacon. Fry tablespoons of the mixture in hot fat until golden brown on both sides. Serve at once. This quantity makes about 8 fritters.

Alternative flavourings to use in the fritters recipe above instead of bacon:

- 2 oz. grated cheese.

- 2-3 oz. finely chopped cooked meat.

- 2-3 oz. flaked cooked fish and 1 tablespoon chopped parsley.

- ½ tin (4½ oz. size) mashed sardines and 1 dessertspoon vinegar.

SAVOURY POTATO CAKES

8 oz. mashed potato
8 oz. cooked fish, flaked
1 tablespoon chopped parsley

1 teaspoon salt
¼ teaspoon pepper

METHOD

Mix all the ingredients well together. Turn on to a board and shape into 4 cakes. Brown under the grill on both sides or bake in a moderate oven till firm and brown.

Alternative flavourings to use instead of the cooked fish in the recipe above:

- **CANNED FISH:** Use 2 oz. sardines, mackerel, pilchards or herrings.

- **BACON:** Omit the salt. Use 2 oz. chopped bacon. Fry the bacon before mixing with the other ingredients. Use the bacon fat for frying the potato cakes.

- **CHEESE AND PARSLEY:** Use only ½ teaspoon salt. Add 1½ oz. grated cheese and 1 tablespoon chopped parsley.

- **MEAT:** Use 2 oz. cooked meat, minced or finely chopped and add 1 teaspoon Worcester sauce.

Pan Hash

8 oz. cooked mashed potatoes
8 oz. mixed cooked
  vegetables, chopped
2 oz. chopped cooked bacon

Salt and pepper
1 oz. fat for frying
  (use the bacon fat)

METHOD

Mix all the ingredients together. Melt the fat in a frying pan and fry the mixture on both sides till well browned, about 15 minutes.

NOTE: If no cooked vegetables are available, 1 lb. cooked mashed potatoes may be used.

Alternative flavourings to use instead of the bacon in the recipe above:

- 2 oz. grated cheese.

- 2 oz. chopped cooked meat.

- 2 oz. flaked cooked fish.

Potato Puffs

For the puffs:
1 lb. cooked mashed potato
Salt and pepper
A little flour

For the fillings:
6 oz. cooked sausage meat,
  or 6 oz. cooked root vegetables,
chopped and 1 oz. grated cheese

METHOD

Mix cold mashed potato with seasoning. Add enough flour to bind the potatoes into a dough which will roll out easily, roll out, cut into 4 fairly large rounds. Season the filling chosen and place a little on each round, dampen edges, fold over and seal. Bake on greased tray or fry in shallow fat.

CHEESE AND VEGETABLE CUTLETS

4 oz. grated cheese   *1 onion, chopped finely*
8 oz. mashed potato   *4 tablespoons flour*
4 oz. cooked peas   *Salt and pepper*
2 carrots, finely grated   *Browned breadcrumbs*

METHOD

Mix together the cheese, vegetables, and flour, and season well. Form into 8 cutlets and coat with browned breadcrumbs. Bake in a moderate oven for 20-25 minutes, or fry in a little fat for 5 minutes, or grill until brown on both sides.

FRIED CHEESE SANDWICHES

2 oz. cheese, sliced   *1 teaspoon made mustard*
4 slices of bread   *Fat for frying*

METHOD

Place the cheese on two of the slices of bread and lightly spread with the mustard. Cover with the remaining slices of bread, cut in two, and fry in hot fat till golden brown on both sides. Serve hot.

POTATO FADGE WITH FRIED BACON

8 oz. cooked mashed potato   *1-2 oz. flour*
Salt and pepper   *4 rashers bacon*

METHOD

Mix potato, seasoning and enough flour to make a stiff dough. Roll out ¼" thick and cut into 8 pieces. Fry bacon and keep hot, then fry the fadge in the bacon fat until brown on both sides. Serve with the bacon.

FRIED HERRINGS

4 filleted or whole herrings   *A little pepper*
2 tablespoons flour or oatmeal   *Fat for frying*
2 teaspoons salt

METHOD

Wipe the fish and dip it in the flour or oatmeal to which the salt and pepper have been added. Heat a little fat in a frying pan until a faint blue haze rises. Put in the fish, and cook until brown on both sides.

NOTE: If whole herrings are used, be sure they are cleaned before cooking.

POACHED KIPPERS

Cut off the heads and tails. Put the fish in a frying pan with just enough cold water to cover. Bring to the boil, simmer for a few minutes. Drain well and serve with a small knob of butter or margarine on each kipper.

NOTE: When available, smoked haddock can also be cooked in this way.

GRILLED FISH

1 tablespoon flour   *2 tablespoons milk*
½ teaspoon salt   *1 lb. fillet of fish, cut in pieces*
Pinch of pepper   *Browned breadcrumbs*
Pinch of grated nutmeg   *1 oz. cooking fat or dripping*

METHOD

Blend the flour, salt, pepper and nutmeg with the milk. Dip the pieces of fish in this and then roll in browned crumbs. Heat the fat in the grill pan and, when hot, dip the fish in it and grill on both sides till brown and cooked. The pieces of coated fish can be baked in a hot oven for ½ hour. Cook in a baking tin or shallow fireproof dish with the fat.

NOTE: The pieces of fish can be sprinkled with salt and pepper and coated in breadcrumbs only.

HARD ROES

These may be washed, dipped in flour or egg and breadcrumbs, and fried in a little hot fat till golden brown.

GRILLED PILCHARDS ON TOAST

1 tin of pilchards (15 oz. size)   *4 slices of buttered toast*

METHOD

Divide the pilchards on to the four slices of toast and place under the grill for several minutes to heat.

FRIED PILCHARDS ON FRIED BREAD

1 tin of pilchards (15 oz. size)   *Fat for frying, if necessary*
4 slices of bread

METHOD

Fry the pilchards till brown on both sides. They should be sufficiently oily to fry without extra fat. Remove from the pan and keep hot. Add a little extra fat if necessary to fry the slices of bread till golden brown on both sides. Divide the pilchards on to the four slices of fried bread and serve hot.

NOTE: Canned herring or sardines may be used instead of pilchards in either of the recipes above.

Easy to Make Soups and Broths

The wartime dieticians were great believers in the idea that the right kind of soups and broths could play an extremely valuable part in creating a truly healthy and nutritious diet. Accordingly, they came up with many imaginative recipes that could either be served in the traditional way before a main meal or even replace a light lunch or dinner.

Explained the Ministry of Food experts: "Once upon a time cooks used to think a good soup needed 3 or 4 hours cooking, and that to be nourishing it must be made from meat and bones. Today we know better. We know that, although meat and bone stocks are tasty, they have very little food value because only the flavour of the meat comes out in the soup. We know, too, that tasty soups can be made quickly using vegetables and vegetable water or stock from meat cubes or vegetable extract. These soups may be made nourishing and sustaining by adding body-building food such as milk, cheese, eggs, fish and meat. Broth is a soup of this kind and is popular with the North Country housewife who prefers to cook some of her meat ration in this way and serve it in place of a meat dish."

The experts also offered good advice, which is still as valid today as it was then, about when to serve soup, suggesting that it could be used as follows:

1) For a mid-morning or late evening snack. Any of the vegetable or cream soups is suitable.

2) As an appetiser at the beginning of dinner. This should be only a light vegetable soup. Do not serve a large portion or the appetite will be spoilt for the main dish that follows.

3) As a main dish. This soup should contain one of the body-building foods such as meat, fish, eggs or cheese. Examples are the recipes for fish soup, Scotch broth, and vegetable broth with dumplings. Alternatively, for supper or lunch, serve a vegetable soup first and follow this with a salad or savoury dish containing one of the body-building foods.

Further advice about soups from the wartime experts:

- It is not necessary to have meat or bone stock to make good soups. Vegetable stock or vegetable water left over after cooking vegetables gives an excellent flavour to any soup, and in addition contains valuable protective substances.

- To make vegetable stock, use the outside leaves and stalks of cabbage, outside stalks of celery, cauliflower stalks, watercress stalks, etc., as well as whole vegetables. Chop or shred the vegetables and put them in enough boiling water to cover. Boil for about half an hour. Strain before using.

- For a quickly made stock, dissolve some meat or yeast extract in boiling water.

- Remember that stock, does not keep very long, especially in hot weather, so be sure to use it up quickly. Do not leave it standing in the saucepan. Empty it into a clean jug or basin.

- Many of the recipes that follow give alternatives of stock or water. It is worthwhile taking the trouble to use stock, which gives a better flavour to the soup.

SCOTCH BROTH (I)

1 oz. pearl barley	*4 tablespoons diced turnip*
2 pints stock	*2 tablespoons diced potato*
2 teaspoons salt	*2 tablespoons chopped onion*
¼ teaspoon pepper	*4 tablespoons shredded cabbage*
6 tablespoons diced carrot	*1 tablespoon chopped parsley*

METHOD

Wash the barley and soak overnight in the water. Place in a pan with the seasoning and bring to the boil, add the carrot, turnip, potato and onion and boil for 40 minutes. Add the cabbage and boil for 10 minutes. Add the parsley just before serving.

SCOTCH BROTH (II)

1 oz. pearl barley
½ lb. boiling beef
2 pints water
½ lb. carrot, diced
1 lb. swede, diced

3 oz. onion or leek, sliced
2 oz. cabbage, sliced
Salt and pepper
1 tablespoon chopped parsley

METHOD

Blanch the barley by pouring on boiling water, leaving a minute or two and then straining. Bring barley, beef and water to boil, skim and simmer for 1 hour. Add the prepared vegetables, except the cabbage, salt and pepper and cook for 1½-2 hours longer, add cabbage 15 minutes before serving. Place chopped parsley in the tureen, pour in the broth (after skimming off any superfluous fat). The meat is served as a separate course. Extra vegetables, cut in large pieces, may be cooked in the broth to serve round the meat.

VEGETABLE SOUP

¾ lb. mixed vegetables
   (including some onion and
   some green vegetables)
½ oz. cooking fat or dripping

1½ pints stock or water
3 teaspoons salt
Good pinch of pepper
3-4 tablespoons grated cheese (optional)

METHOD

Prepare and shred or slice the vegetables. Heat the fat or dripping and add the vegetables. Cover with a lid and cook gently without browning for 15-20 minutes, shaking the pan occasionally to prevent sticking. Add the liquid and seasoning and boil gently until the vegetables are tender. For variety, 1 oz. of macaroni, spaghetti, or noodles, may be added with the liquid. Serve the cheese separately to be sprinkled on the soup according to taste.

Tomato Soup

½ oz. cooking fat or dripping	2 pints boiling stock or water
3 oz. carrot, sliced	1 lb. fresh or canned tomatoes
4 oz. potato, sliced	1 tablespoon salt
Piece of leek or celery, sliced	¼ teaspoon pepper
2 or 3 bacon rinds	2 oz. flour

METHOD

Heat the fat or dripping in a saucepan and fry the carrot, potato, leek or celery and bacon rinds for a few minutes. Pour on the boiling stock or water, add the sliced tomatoes and seasoning and boil gently until the vegetables are tender. Remove the bacon rinds and mash with a wooden spoon, or put through a sieve. Thicken with the flour, blended with a little cold stock or water. If it can be spared, a tablespoon of sugar improves the flavour of this soup.

Beetroot and Cabbage Soup

2 pints water	2 cloves
1 lb. beetroot, grated coarsely	3 tablespoons flour
½ lb. cabbage, shredded	A little grated cheese
Salt and pepper	Chopped parsley
2 teaspoons vinegar	

METHOD

Bring the water to the boil, add the beetroot and boil gently for 10 minutes. Add the cabbage and season well, adding the vinegar and cloves Cover the pan and boil gently until tender, about 15 minutes. Blend the flour with a little cold water and stir it into the soup. Boil 5 minutes. Serve sprinkled with grated cheese and chopped parsley.

French Peasant Soup

2 pints vegetable stock or water	*¹/₄ teaspoon pepper*
1 lb. mixed root vegetables,	*2 oz. stale breadcrumbs*
diced (including potatoes)	*2 oz. grated cheese*
1 tablespoon salt	*2 tablespoons coarsely chopped parsley*

METHOD

Bring the stock or water to the boil and add the diced vegetables, salt and pepper. Boil gently until tender, and stir in the breadcrumbs, grated cheese and parsley. Serve at once.

Parsnip or Swede Soup

2 pints water or stock	*Salt and pepper*
1¹/₄ lb. parsnips or swede,	*2 tablespoons flour*
peeled and shredded	*4 tablespoons milk*
2 oz. leek or onion	*2 tablespoons chopped parsley*

METHOD

Put water or stock in a pan and bring to boil. When boiling, add shredded parsnips or swedes, chopped leek or onion and seasoning. Boil for 20 minutes. Mix flour to a smooth paste with a little water. Add to soup, reboil, stirring to prevent lumps. Cook for 5 minutes. Add milk and reheat but do not reboil. Stir in coarsely chopped parsley just before serving.

CHEESE AND POTATO SOUP

1½ lb. potatoes	*1 oz. flour*
1 stick celery	*2 oz. grated cheese*
3 oz. onion or leek	*2 tablespoons chopped parsley*
2 pints vegetable stock or water	

METHOD

Scrub and slice potatoes and celery. Peel and slice onion or leek. Place vegetables in boiling water or stock. Cook with the lid on till quite soft. Rub through a sieve or mash well with a wooden spoon. Blend the flour with a little water. Add to the soup, bring to the boil again, and boil 5 minutes. Add the cheese and parsley and serve.

KALE AND POTATO SOUP

2 pints stock or water	*4 oz. kale shredded*
1½ lb. potatoes,	*4 tablespoons household milk, dry*
* peeled and chopped*	*Salt and pepper*
3 oz. onion or leek, chopped	*Chopped parsley*

METHOD

Boil half the stock or water and add the potatoes and onion or leek. Boil until the vegetables are soft, then mash. Bring to the boil again and add the washed and shredded kale. Cook for a further half hour. Mix the milk with the rest of the water and reheat. Season with salt and pepper and sprinkle with chopped parsley before serving.

CABBAGE SOUP

1 oz. dripping or cooking fat
4 oz. shredded cabbage
1 medium-sized onion, chopped
3 oz. carrot, grated

1 oz. oatmeal
1 pint stock or water
Pinch of pepper
1 pint milk

METHOD

Melt the dripping or fat in a saucepan and fry the vegetables gently for about 5 minutes, without browning. Add the cabbage and oatmeal and cook for a further 3 minutes. Add the stock or water and seasoning. Boil gently for 20 minutes. Lastly, add the milk and reheat.

NOTE: Any vegetable can be used instead of the cabbage, according to the season, for example, beetroot, artichoke, etc.

WATERCRESS SOUP

¼ oz. cooking fat or dripping
4 oz. leek, sliced
1 oz. watercress, chopped
1 lb. potatoes, cut in quarters
1 pint water

2 teaspoons salt
¼ teaspoon pepper
2 or 3 bacon rinds
½ pint milk

METHOD

Heat the fat or dripping in a pan and add the sliced leek, half the watercress and the potatoes. Fry gently without browning for about 5 minutes. Add the water, salt, pepper and bacon rinds. Boil gently until the potatoes are soft, then mash with a wooden spoon. Remove bacon rinds, add the milk and, just before serving, the remainder of the watercress.

Purée for Cream of Vegetable Soup

To make ½ pint of purée for the cream of vegetable soup recipe that follows, use one of the following:

1 lb. any root vegetable; or
¾ lb. potatoes and ½ lb. watercress; or
½ lb. tomatoes; or
2 lb. marrow or cucumber; or
6 oz. dried peas

METHOD

Whichever vegetable is used, cook it until tender in ½ pint of boiling salted water. The dried peas should be soaked overnight before cooking. Rub the cooked vegetables through a sieve and keep hot until required. If not quite ½ pint purée is obtained, make it up with hot water.

Cream of Vegetable Soup

½ pint vegetable purée (see above)   *1 oz. flour*
½ oz. margarine or dripping   *1 pint milk or milk and water*
2 tablespoons chopped   *Salt and pepper to taste*
* parsley or watercress*

METHOD

Melt the margarine or dripping and stir in the flour. Mix until smooth. Add the milk or milk and water and stir until boiling. Boil 5 minutes. Then add the hot vegetable purée just before serving. Mix well and season to taste. Sprinkle with the parsley or watercress just before serving.

QUICK SOUP

2 oz. cabbage
2 oz. onion
4 oz. mixed root vegetables
½ oz. cooking fat or dripping
2 pints water

1 teaspoon meat extract
2 teaspoons salt
Pinch of pepper
1 tablespoon chopped parsley

METHOD

Prepare vegetables. Shred the cabbage finely, chop the onion and grate the root vegetables. Melt the fat or dripping and fry the vegetables gently for about 5 minutes. Pour the liquid on to the vegetables, add seasoning and meat extract. Boil gently for 10-15 minutes, sprinkle with parsley and serve at once.

ONION SOUP AU GRATIN

½ oz. dripping or other fat
4 small onions (½ lb.),
    thinly sliced
2 pints hot stock
    (4 beef cubes and water)

3 teaspoons salt
¼ teaspoon pepper
4 slices thin toast
4 tablespoons grated cheese

METHOD

Heat the dripping or fat and fry the sliced onions until soft. Add the hot stock and seasoning, bring to the boil and boil gently for 5-10 minutes. Place the toast at the bottom of the soup plates, sprinkle with grated cheese and pour on the hot soup.

If preferred, grated cheese and dry toast may be handed separately with the soup instead of placing it in the plates.

FISH SOUP

1 lb. fish (haddock if possible)	*1 oz. margarine*
½ lb. fish trimmings	*2 oz. flour*
2 pints water	*½ pint milk*
3 oz. onion or leek	*Salt and pepper*
2 cloves	*1 tablespoon chopped parsley*

METHOD

Wash and clean the fish and trimmings. Place in a pan with the water, onion or leek and cloves. Bring to the boil and skim well. Cook gently for 10 minutes. Lift out the fish. Remove the skin and flake the fish. Cook the stock for half hour longer. Strain the stock and rinse the pan. Melt the margarine, add the flour and cook for a few minutes, add the stock and milk and stir until boiling. Add the flaked fish, season and boil gently for 5 minutes. Add the chopped parsley and serve.

VEGETABLE BROTH WITH SAUSAGE DUMPLINGS

For the dumplings:	*For the broth:*
4 oz. self-raising flour	*½ lb. carrot*
or 4 oz. plain flour and	*3 oz. turnip*
2 teaspoons baking powder	*3 oz. onion or leek*
1 teaspoon salt	*4 oz. chopped outer cabbage leaves*
1 oz. chopped suet or dripping	*½ lb. potatoes*
1 tablespoon chopped parsley	*2 pints stock*
4 oz. sausage meat	
Water to mix	

METHOD

Chop onions or leek, carrots, cabbage, turnip and potatoes, place in the boiling stock and boil gently for half hour. Make dumplings by mixing together all ingredients. If dripping is used it should be rubbed into flour before mixing in other ingredients. Mix with cold water to a fairly stiff consistency and cut into 8 small pieces. Roll into balls and dip in flour. Add to broth, which must be boiling and boil gently for 20 minutes.

Meat-Based Main Meals

SAUSAGE ROLL

8 oz. sausage meat
2 tablespoons finely
    chopped onion or leek
1 tablespoon chopped pickle
3 oz. breadcrumbs

Pinch of mixed herbs
Pinch of pepper
1½ teaspoons salt
2 tablespoons stock or milk

METHOD

Mix all the ingredients together thoroughly. Turn into a greased tin. Cover with lid and steam 1½-2 hours.

GRAVY FOR THE SAUSAGE ROLL ABOVE

3 tablespoons flour
Pinch of pepper
½ pint vegetable water

1 meat cube
Gravy browning

METHOD

Blend the flour and pepper with a little cold water, pour on the vegetable water and return to the pan with the meat cube. Bring to the boil, stirring all the time and boil for 5 minutes. Add gravy browning and salt if necessary.

Hot Pot

½ oz. dripping or cooking fat
2 oz. chopped onions
4 lamb chops
1 lb. potatoes, sliced thinly
8 oz. carrots, sliced
8 oz. turnips, sliced

Pinch of mixed herbs
2 teaspoons salt
¼ teaspoon pepper
½ pint water or stock
8 oz. finely shredded cabbage

METHOD

Melt the dripping or fat and fry the onions and chops on both sides for about 5 minutes. Lift out the chops and put in the mixed vegetables, herbs, salt, pepper and liquid, put the chops back on top. Cover the pan and simmer for 30 minutes. Add the cabbage and cook for a further 10-15 minutes.

Braised Meat

2 lb. stewing beef
1 oz. cooking fat or dripping
1½ lb. mixed root vegetables

2 teaspoons salt
1 teaspoon pepper
½ pint stock or water

METHOD

Roll the meat and tie securely or cut it into neat pieces. Heat the fat or dripping and brown the meat on both sides. Remove the meat from the pan, strain off any fat and add the vegetables. Add the seasoning and liquid, then place the meat on top of the vegetables, put on the lid and boil gently for 2 hours.

Bacon Hot Pot

1-1½ lb. potatoes,
   cut in thin slices
2 oz. onions, finely chopped
3 oz. bacon, finely chopped
2 tablespoons chopped parsley

2-3 teaspoons salt
½ teaspoon pepper
¼ pint stock
8 oz. shredded cabbage

METHOD

Grease a cake tin or pudding basin. Arrange layers of potatoes, onion, bacon and parsley in it, seasoning each layer. Add the stock, cover with a plate or a piece of greased paper and steam for 1½ hours. 15 minutes before serving, arrange cabbage round tin or basin to steam.

Braised Lamb Chops

4 lamb chops
½ oz. fat or
   dripping for frying
3 bacon rinds
8 oz. mixed vegetables, diced
8 tomatoes, sliced
1 teaspoon salt
Pinch of pepper
¼-½ pint stock or water

Flavourings:
1 clove, 1 blade mace,
or 3 peppercorns,
tiny sprig of thyme,
1 or 2 leaves of mint

METHOD

Trim all the surplus fat from the chops. Heat the fat or dripping and bacon rinds in a pan and fry the chops until well browned on both sides. Remove from the pan and pour off the fat. Place the vegetables in the pan with the tomatoes, flavourings, seasoning and stock or water. Lay the chops on the vegetables, cover the pan with a lid. Cook very gently for about ³/₄ hour. Remove the bacon rinds and serve the chops on a hot dish with the vegetables and gravy.

WHITE STEW

1 lb. scrag end	*1 bay leaf*
or middle neck of lamb	*³/₄ pint stock or water*
or ³/₄ lb. pork or veal	*3 teaspoons salt*
8 oz. onions	*¹/₄ teaspoon pepper*
4 oz. carrots	*4 tablespoons flour*
3 oz. turnips	*1 tablespoon chopped parsley*

METHOD

Cut the meat into suitable sized pieces for serving and put into a saucepan with the peeled and sliced vegetables, stock or water and seasoning. Simmer for 1½-2 hours, stirring occasionally. Mix the flour to a smooth paste with a little cold water. Add some of the hot gravy from the stew, mix well and return to the saucepan and stir until it boils. Boil for 5 minutes. Serve hot, sprinkled with chopped parsley.

CORNED BEEF HASH

1 can condensed oxtail soup	*1 tablespoon onion flakes*
4 oz. packet dried	*12 oz. canned corned beef, diced*
mixed vegetables	*Salt*
4 medium-sized potatoes,	*Pepper*
peeled and sliced	

METHOD

Make the soup up to ³/₄ pint by adding water to it in a saucepan. Bring to the boil, stirring well, then add the vegetables and simmer for 10 minutes or until they are tender. Add the corned beef, salt and pepper and cook for a further 5 minutes.

BROWN STEW

1 lb. stewing meat
  (beef, lamb, veal, or pork)
4 tablespoons flour
3 teaspoons salt
1 teaspoon pepper

1 oz. cooking fat or dripping
8 oz. onions, sliced
8 oz. root vegetables, sliced
Small piece of bay leaf
¾ pint water

METHOD

Cut the meat into pieces (about 1" cubes) and roll in the flour and seasoning until well coated. Melt the fat or dripping in a saucepan and fry the meat until a good brown colour. Add the vegetables to the meat with the bay leaf and water. Simmer for 1½-2 hours, or until tender.

MEAT CURRY

1 small onion
1 medium-sized apple
1½ oz. dripping
¾-1 lb. beef or lamb
1½ tablespoons
  curry powder
4 tablespoons flour
½ teaspoon dry mustard

¾ pint stock or water
1 teaspoon sugar
1 tablespoon chutney
  or vinegar
1 tablespoon marmalade
1 teaspoon black treacle
  or syrup
2 teaspoons salt

METHOD

Chop the onion and the apple finely and fry in the melted dripping. Add the meat in 1" cubes and fry lightly. Remove the meat from the frying pan and work in the curry powder, flour and dry mustard. Cook for 2-3 minutes, add the liquid gradually and bring to the boil, stirring all the time. Add the sugar, chutney, marmalade, black treacle or syrup and salt. Replace the meat and simmer for 1-1½ hours, or until tender. In place of rice serve either macaroni, barley or potatoes with the curry.

DUMPLINGS (TO ADD BULK TO STEWS)

4 oz. plain flour and
2 teaspoons baking powder
or 4 oz. self-raising flour

1 teaspoon salt
Milk to mix, about 3-4 tablespoons

METHOD

Mix the dry ingredients together. Add enough milk to mix to soft dough. Cut mixture into 8 portions and shape roughly into dumplings with the hands. Drop into the stew and cook for 10-15 minutes with the lid on.

MINCE-IN-THE-HOLE

For the mince:
4 oz. minced meat,
fresh or cooked (beef, pork,
lamb, or veal)
1 leek, chopped finely
2 teaspoons mixed herbs
1 teaspoon salt
Pinch of pepper
½ oz. cooking fat or dripping

For the batter:
4 oz. flour
1 or 2 eggs
½ teaspoon salt
Pinch of pepper

METHOD

Mix the mince, leek, herbs and seasoning together. Form into meatballs. Melt the fat in a baking pan, put in meatballs and put in the oven to heat. Mix the flour, eggs, salt and pepper to a thick batter with some of the liquid, beat well, add more liquid to make a thin batter and heat again. Pour this over meatballs and bake in a hot oven for 30-45 minutes.

HAMBURGERS

8 oz. minced beef
4 oz. stale bread,
   soaked and squeezed
Pinch of herbs
2 teaspoons salt

1/3 teaspoon pepper
1/4 teaspoon mustard
4 teaspoons Worcester sauce
2 tablespoons chopped onion
1 egg (optional)

METHOD

Mix all the ingredients together and form into 8 rounds. Fry in shallow fat for 15 minutes or until cooked in the middle. Put a large saucepan lid over the frying pan during cooking as this conserves the heat. Serve with potatoes and watercress or raw salad.

HAMBURGERS IN BROWN SAUCE

Use hamburger recipe as above
Sauce:
2 oz. dripping
1 small onion, chopped
1 1/2 oz. flour
1 pint water or stock
Gravy browning
1/2 teaspoon salt

1/4 teaspoon pepper
1 teaspoon sugar
1 teaspoon vinegar
1 teaspoon chutney
2 tablespoons diced carrot
2 tablespoons diced potato

METHOD

Melt the dripping and fry the hamburgers until brown but not cooked through. Remove from the pan. Fry the onion until brown. Add the flour and mix well. Add the liquid gradually, stirring until the sauce boils. Add the other ingredients and the hamburgers, cover and simmer for 15-20 minutes.

SAVOURY MEAT PUDDING

For the pastry:
8 oz. plain flour
2 teaspoons baking powder
½ teaspoon salt
1 oz. suet or cooking fat
1 oz. grated raw potato
Water to mix

For the filling:
9 oz. minced or chopped beef,
pork, lamb, or veal
3 tablespoons flour
1 lb. diced vegetables
3 tablespoons chopped leek
or onion
1-2 teaspoons salt
Pinch of pepper
¼ pint stock
Gravy browning

METHOD

Mix the flour, baking powder and salt. Rub in the fat or suet and mix in the grated potato. Mix to a stiff dough with cold water. Line the basin with ³/₄ of the pastry. Mix the meat with the flour. Arrange layers of the vegetables, leek, meat and seasoning in the basin. Add the stock in which a little gravy browning has been mixed. Roll out the rest of the pastry to fit the top. Press the edges together. Cover with greased paper and steam for 2½-3 hours.

Making the Meat Go Further with Stuffing

Always seeking ways to make the most of the very limited amount of meat available on rations, the wartime Ministry of Food came up with several suggestions for various stuffings, explaining: "Stuffing can stretch the meat in two ways. By adding to the bulk and by adding a body-building food such as an egg in the recipe below. The stuffing can either be cooked in the meat or formed into balls to cook round the joint or in a separate pan. Both slow roasting and braising are good ways of cooking a stuffed joint."

MINT STUFFING

6 oz. stale bread,
  soaked and squeezed
4 tablespoons chopped onion
6-8 tablespoons chopped mint
1-2 tablespoons vinegar

1 tablespoon sugar
2 teaspoons salt
2 teaspoons bacon fat
1 egg

METHOD

Mix all the ingredients together and use to stuff lamb or mutton.

FORCEMEAT STUFFING

6 oz. stale bread,
  soaked and squeezed
2 tablespoons chopped parsley
1 teaspoon mixed herbs

2 teaspoons salt
½ teaspoon pepper
½ oz. dripping, cooking fat,
  or bacon fat

METHOD

Mix together the bread, parsley, herbs, and seasoning. Melt the dripping or fat, and add to the dry ingredients. Mix thoroughly. Use as required.

APPLE AND CELERY STUFFING

6 oz. stale bread,
  soaked and squeezed
3 oz. chopped onion
6 oz. chopped celery
3 oz. chopped apple

2 teaspoons salt
½ teaspoon pepper
2 teaspoons sage
Water to mix

METHOD

Bind the ingredients together with a little water and use as required.

RHUBARB AND RAISIN STUFFING

6 oz. stale crusts,
  soaked and squeezed
½ oz. suet, dripping, or bacon fat
2-3 oz. chopped rhubarb

2 tablespoons chopped raisins
2 teaspoons salt
Pinch of pepper
1 teaspoon thyme

METHOD

Mix all the ingredients together. If using dripping or bacon fat, melt this before adding it to the dry ingredients. Use for stuffing pork, lamb or veal.

Fish-Based Main Meals

Although fish was not rationed, many of the fish we take for granted nowadays – such as cod, haddock and even salmon – either were simply not available during World War II or were in extremely short supply, this due in great part to the fact that many of the men who had manned the fishing fleets had been drafted. To make matters even worse, many of the traditional fishing grounds were also unsafe because of German naval activity.

As a result of these two factors, herring became the main fish food source and, as you'll see below, the Ministry of Food came up with many ingenious ways of making this rather mundane fish altogether more exciting.

Fish Stew

1 lb. white fish	*2 teaspoons salt*
8 oz. onions, sliced	*½ teaspoon pepper*
8 oz. tomatoes, sliced	*½ pint water*
1½ lb. potatoes,	*2 tablespoons flour*
peeled and cut into chunks	

METHOD

Remove any skin and bone from the fish and cut into 1" cubes. Place in a pan with the vegetables, seasoning, and water. Simmer gently for 30 minutes. Blend the flour with a little water and add to the stew, stirring all the time. Cook for 5 minutes, then serve in a hot dish.

Baked Herrings

4 herrings, boiled	*A few peppercorns*
2 small onions if liked	*Salt*
(cut into slices)	

METHOD

Season the insides of the fillets with a little salt, and roll each piece round a piece of onion. Pack closely into a greased pie dish or casserole. Sprinkle the top with salt and a few peppercorns. Cover with a piece of greaseproof paper and bake in a moderate oven for about 10 minutes. Then remove the paper, and allow the fish to brown for a further 5 minutes.

BAKED STUFFED HERRINGS

4 herrings, boned
For the stuffing:

2 oz. breadcrumbs
* or stale bread, soaked*
* and squeezed*
½ oz. melted dripping
* or other fat*

2 tablespoons chopped parsley
1 strip lemon rind, if available
½ teaspoon thyme
1 dried egg (reconstituted)
Salt and pepper

METHOD

Mix together the bread, parsley, chopped lemon rind, and thyme and season well. Add the fat. Bind with the egg. Season the insides of the fish with salt and pepper, spread with stuffing and fold back into shape. Lay them in a greased fireproof dish and bake in a moderate oven for about 10 minutes.

DEVILLED HERRINGS

4 herrings, boned
2 dessertspoons mustard
* mixed with vinegar*
1 tablespoon sugar
1 oz. margarine

1 onion chopped finely
1 bay leaf
6 cloves
¼ pint water

METHOD

Mix the mustard, sugar and half the margarine to a paste. Spread on the herrings and roll up. Fry the onion, the bay leaf and the cloves in the remaining half-ounce of margarine in a saucepan, add the rolled up herrings and the water, and simmer gently for 10 minutes. Baste herrings occasionally with the liquid. When cooked, serve with sweet chutney.

HERRING AND TOMATO DISH

4 herrings, boned
½ lb. tomatoes, fresh or bottled
1 oz. cooking fat or dripping
4 cloves
1 bay leaf

3 tablespoons plain flour
½ pint milk or vegetable stock
2 teaspoons mustard
1 lb. cooked mashed potato

METHOD

Cut the herrings into pieces. Place in a greased casserole dish with the tomatoes (skinned and sliced fresh). Melt the fat, fry the cloves and bay leaf in it for 2-3 minutes, add the flour, and the liquid. Bring to the boil, and boil for 2-3 minutes. Add the mustard, season well, and pour over the contents in the dish. Cover with the potato and bake for ½ hour in a moderate oven.

STEAMED HERRINGS
(SUITABLE FOR WHOLE OR BONED FISH)

METHOD

Place the fish to be steamed on a plate over a pan of boiling water. Put knob or two of margarine or dripping on the fish. Cover with a pan lid or an inverted plate, and cook until the fish is tender, 10-15 minutes. Serve with one of the sauces below.

SAUCES FOR STEAMED HERRINGS RECIPE
(BUT WHICH ARE ALSO SUITABLE FOR USE WITH A
WIDE VARIETY OF OTHER HERRING AND FISH RECIPES):

Foundation Melted Butter Sauce

1 oz. margarine
2 tablespoons plain flour

1 pint hot water

Melt the margarine and mix in the flour. Cook for 2-3 minutes. Pour in the hot water, bring gradually to the boil, and boil very gently for 2-3 minutes. Add seasoning and capers, fennel or mustard, as suggested below.

Caper Sauce

Add 1 tablespoon capers, or pickled nasturtium seeds cut in two, or coarsely chopped, and 1 dessertspoon vinegar from the capers to ½ pint foundation sauce.

Fennel Sauce

Add 2 tablespoons chopped fennel to ½ pint foundation sauce.

Mustard Sauce

Mix together 2 teaspoons mustard and 2 teaspoons vinegar, and stir into ½ pint foundation sauce.

QUICK SOUSED HERRINGS

4 herrings, boned
1 dessertspoon pickling spice
1 bay leaf
Salt

Small amount of
*   sliced onion or spring onion*
⅓ pint water
⅓ pint vinegar

METHOD

Place the fish, either flat or rolled up in a frying pan or saucepan (preferably aluminium or enamel). Sprinkle with the spices, broken bay leaf, and onion, then cover with the vinegar and water. Cover the frying pan with a lid, or an enamel plate to fit tightly. Heat slowly, and keep the pan just simmering for about 20 minutes to ½ hour. Then remove from the liquor, and serve the fish hot, or leave the fish to cool in a covered pan if they are to be served cold with salad.

HERRING SALAD

4 boned, flaked cooked herrings	2 tablespoons raw grated
1½ lb. sliced cooked potatoes	turnip or swede
1 small onion or leek,	Salt and pepper
finely chopped	4 tablespoons salad dressing
2 tomatoes, sliced	½ lb. shredded raw cabbage heart
6 prunes, soaked 24 hours	2 tablespoons chopped parsley
and chopped	

METHOD

Mix all ingredients except cabbage and parsley with sufficient dressing to moisten well. Pile on a bed of shredded cabbage and sprinkle with chopped parsley.

PICKLED HERRINGS

This recipe obviously makes considerably more than the usual 'sufficient for four' quantity and could be made to stretch for up to 20 servings.

1 pint vinegar	2 level teaspoons allspice
1 pint water	4-5 onions, sliced
Salt to taste	4 slices lemon, if available
20 peppercorns	20 herrings (approx.)
5 bay leaves	

METHOD

Boil the vinegar with the water, salt, peppercorns, broken up bay leaves, allspice, and onions for half an hour. Add the slices of lemon and boil for five minutes longer. Simmer the fish in the liquid until it is soft. As they are done, pack them in a stone jar with one or two thin slices of raw onion between each layer of fish. When the jar is full, cover with the hot liquid without straining it. Store in a cool place and the fish will jellify, and keep for several weeks.

SOUSED HERRINGS

8 herrings, boned   *½ pint vinegar*
1 onion, sliced   *½ pint water*
1 tablespoon mixed   *1 teaspoon salt*
 pickling spice

METHOD

Roll up the fish with a slice of onion inside each fish, Pack in a baking dish. Scatter pickling spice between the rolls, and add the remainder of the sliced onion. Sprinkle in salt, pour in vinegar and water mixed together, and bake in a slow oven for 1¼ hours.

HERRING PIE

1 lb. grated raw potato   *Salt and pepper*
1 lb. grated raw apple   *4 herrings, boned*
1 onion, chopped   *1 teaspoon lemon substitute*
¼ teaspoon nutmeg   *6 oz. pastry*

METHOD

Grease a shallow dish and arrange half the potato, apple and onion on it. Sprinkle on the nutmeg seasoning and lemon substitute. Lay the herrings on top. Cover with the remainder of the potato, apple and onion mixture. Roll out the pastry. Cover the dish with it, and bake in a hot oven for 30 minutes.

HERRING ROE SAVOURY

8 soft roes	*4 slices of toast*
¼ pint milk	*Salt and pepper*
1½ tablespoons plain flour	*Chopped parsley*

METHOD

Rinse roes. Stew in the milk until they are tender, about 10-15 minutes. Place 2 roes on each piece of toast and keep hot. Mix the flour to a smooth paste with a little cold water, add the boiled milk. Return to the saucepan and stir until boiling. Boil 5 minutes, season well, and pour over the roes. Garnish with chopped parsley.

MOCK OYSTER PUDDING

5 medium soft roes	*2 dried eggs (reconstituted)*
2 oz. dried breadcrumbs	*1 teaspoon sugar*
1 pint milk	*Salt and pepper*
1 oz. melted margarine	*A little nutmeg*

METHOD

Rinse the roes, and drain well. Chop finely. Mix with the breadcrumbs, milk, margarine, eggs, sugar, seasoning and nutmeg. Turn into a greased pie dish. Bake till golden brown in a moderately hot oven for about 30 minutes.

Cheese-Based Main Meals

VEGETABLE PIE WITH CHEESE AND OATMEAL CRUST

1½ lb. cooked,
  mixed vegetables
2 tablespoons
  chopped parsley
1 pint stock or water

For the pastry:
2 oz. oatmeal
4 oz. flour
2 oz. mashed potato
1 oz. fat
2 oz. cheese
Water to mix
Salt

METHOD

Place cooked vegetables in a pie dish and sprinkle with coarsely chopped parsley. Add vegetable water and seasoning. To make the pastry, cream fat and potato together. Mix grated cheese, oatmeal, flour and salt and stir into the creamed fat and potato. Mix to a stiff dough with water. Roll out the pastry, cover the pie and bake in a moderate oven for 30 minutes. Serve with baked jacket potatoes and greens.

CHEESE SAVOURY

1 dried egg (reconstituted)
½ pint milk, household milk
  or vegetable stock
Salt, pepper and mustard

1 breakfast cup
  or 4 oz. breadcrumbs
4 oz. grated cheese

METHOD

Reconstitute the egg and beat up with the milk. Add the other ingredients. Pour into a greased dish and bake for 20 minutes in a moderate oven until brown and set. Serve with baked jacket potatoes, mashed swedes and watercress.

POTATO JANE

2 lb. potatoes
2 oz. breadcrumbs or oatmeal
½ chopped leek
½-¾ pint milk and water

4 oz. grated cheese
1 sliced carrot
Salt and pepper

METHOD

Put a layer of sliced potato in a fireproof dish. Sprinkle with some of the leek, carrot, crumbs or oatmeal, cheese and seasoning. Fill dish with alternate layers, finishing with a layer of mixed cheese and breadcrumbs, or oatmeal. Pour over the milk, cover with a lid or greased paper and bake in a moderate oven for ¾-1 hour or steam for 1-1½ hours. Serve with mashed carrots and swedes, sprinkled with coarsely chopped parsley.

CHEESE OMELETTE

4 dried eggs (reconstituted)
Salt and pepper

2 oz. grated cheese
Fat

METHOD

Beat eggs with seasoning. Heat sufficient fat in a pan to grease the bottom, rub the surplus fat round the sides of the pan. Pour in ¼ of the egg mixture, to cover the bottom, and shake well, using a fork to loosen the sides. When the eggs are set, sprinkle with cheese and fold in half. Serve on to a hot plate and sprinkle with parsley or garnish with watercress or shredded raw cabbage. Repeat this process, making 4 omelettes in all.

CHEESE POTATOES

2 lb. potatoes	Pinch of pepper
4 oz. grated cheese	½ teaspoon dry mustard
2 teaspoons salt	4 tablespoons milk

METHOD

Cook the potatoes until soft, drain and mash well. Beat in the cheese, seasoning and milk. Serve immediately.

Egg-Based Main Meals

BACON AND EGG PIE

This one still remains a favourite to this day, often offered as a light lunch in many pubs.

2 dried eggs (reconstituted)	2 oz. mashed potato
2 rashers grilled bacon	Salt and pepper
8 oz. potato pastry	

METHOD

Beat the eggs. Line a plate with half the pastry. Mix the eggs, potato, salt and pepper, and chopped bacon together. Pour this mixture on to the plate, cover with the rest of the pastry. Bake in a moderate oven for ½ hour. Serve hot with vegetables or cold with salad.

OMELETTE

2 dried eggs (reconstituted)	Salt and pepper
½-¾ oz. margarine or fat	

METHOD

Beat the eggs and salt and pepper. Heat fat in the pan, pour in the eggs and work them with a fork in the usual manner. Fold over and serve immediately.

SPANISH OMELETTE (VARIATION OF THE ABOVE)

2 dried eggs (reconstituted)
8 oz. grated mixed vegetables
Small piece of
   chopped leek or parsley

2 tablespoons water
Salt and pepper
1½ oz. margarine or dripping

METHOD

Beat the eggs. Heat the fat in a frying pan and fry the vegetables and leek until tender. Add the eggs, water and seasoning. Stir until the eggs are set, then shape into a crescent, and serve immediately. Or serve flat without folding.

Vegetarian Main Dish

LORD WOOLTON PIE

Created during World War II by a chef at the Savoy to prove that a truly satisfying main dish could be produced without meat or fish, this dish was named in honour of Lord Woolton, the at the time Minister of Food.

8 oz. plain shortcrust pastry
2 tablespoons finely
   chopped fresh sage
1½ lb. mixed root vegetables,
   such as turnip, carrot,
   potato and swede, peeled
   and finely chopped
Salt and freshly ground
   black pepper
6 spring onions, chopped

2 onions, finely chopped
3 tablespoons finely chopped
   fresh parsley
4 oz. butter
2 heaped tablespoons plain flour
¾ pint milk
6 oz. Cheddar cheese, grated,
   plus a little extra to sprinkle on top
½ teaspoon English mustard
Fresh parsley sprigs, to garnish

METHOD

Roll out the pastry on a lightly floured surface sprinkled with 1 tablespoon chopped sage and use it to line a deep 9" tart tin.

Prebake or bake blind. Preheat the oven to moderate heat. Cook the vegetables in a pan of lightly salted, boiling water for a few minutes only, or until just soft. Drain, return the vegetables to the pan, add the spring onions, onions, parsley, remaining sage and salt and pepper and mix well. Spoon the vegetable mixture into the pre-baked pastry case and set aside. Melt the butter in a pan, stir in the flour and cook for 1 minute, stirring to ensure the flour has cooked properly. Gradually stir in the milk, then bring slowly to the boil, stirring until the sauce thickens. Stir in the cheese, mustard and salt and pepper to taste. Pour the cheese sauce over the vegetables in the pastry case and sprinkle a little grated cheese on top. Bake in the oven for 35-40 minutes or until the surface is set and nicely browned. Serve hot with a green vegetable and garnish with a sprig or two of parsley.

NOTE: The quantities above will provide a main meal for 6-8, but this pie is also an excellent dish to accompany a roast meal, making it perfect for Sunday lunch. As an accompaniment, it will serve 10-12.

Vegetables

PIQUANT SPINACH

3 lb. spinach
1½ rashers bacon

2 teaspoons salt
3 teaspoons horseradish sauce

METHOD

Wash and prepare the spinach. Chop bacon and fry till golden brown. Add spinach and salt and moisten with a little water. Cook until tender. Strain and chop well. Mix in horseradish and serve at once.

BEANS BÉARNAISE

1 lb. runner beans
Small knob of fat
1 oz. bacon, chopped

2 tomatoes, chopped
Salt and pepper

METHOD

Break beans into short lengths and cook until tender in a little boiling salted water. Drain and keep hot. Place fat in pan and fry bacon and tomatoes. When cooked, add the beans and mix well. Season and serve.

BROCCOLI OR CAULIFLOWER WITH HOLLANDAISE SAUCE

1 large or 2 small broccoli heads
*   or cauliflowers*
2 tablespoons flour
1 pint milk or stock,
*   or vegetable water*

4 peppercorns (in muslin bag)
2 dried eggs (reconstituted)
3 tablespoons vinegar
Pepper and salt

METHOD

Separate broccoli or cauliflower into small pieces and boil until tender in a little salted water. Drain. Mix the flour to a smooth paste with a little of the milk or stock, boil remainder, pour on to flour, return to pan, stir until it boils, and boil 5 minutes with the peppercorns. Remove from heat and add the eggs carefully, boil 2-3 minutes longer. Remove the peppercorns, add vinegar and seasoning and pour over the broccoli or cauliflower.

Brussels Sprouts a L'Italienne

1 lb. Brussels sprouts	*Salt and pepper*
Salt	*Pinch of grated nutmeg*
1 oz. margarine	*Lemon substitute*
1 oz. flour	*2-3 oz. grated cheese*
1 pint milk and vegetable water	

METHOD

Wash and clean the sprouts, cook in a little boiling salted water until tender. Drain, keeping the vegetable water. Melt the fat, add the flour and cook for about 2 minutes. Add the liquid, bring to the boil and cook for 5 minutes. Add seasoning to taste, grated nutmeg, a few drops of lemon substitute and grated cheese. Mix thoroughly. Add the sprouts to the sauce and heat through. Serve hot.

Red Cabbage

1 oz. fat or dripping	*2 tablespoons stock or water*
1 lb. red cabbage, shredded	*1 tablespoon vinegar*
1 large onion, sliced	*Salt and pepper*
1 large apple, sliced	*2 teaspoons sugar, brown if possible*

METHOD

Melt the fat in a saucepan and add all the other ingredients. Cover with a tightly fitting lid and boil gently until the cabbage is tender, about 30-40 minutes. Shake the pan occasionally during cooking to prevent the cabbage from sticking. Do not cook over a fierce heat or the cabbage will boil dry. This is excellent served with pork or with grilled or fried sausages.

Salads

Please note that all vegetables and fruit in the recipes are raw unless otherwise stated.

COLESLAW

8 oz. finely shredded cabbage heart
3 tablespoons finely chopped onion
About ¼ pint salad dressing

METHOD

Shred the cabbage heart as fine as matchsticks, mix with the onion and dressing and turn into a salad bowl. Chopped chives may be used instead of the onion or the bowl can be rubbed round with garlic before the cabbage is placed in it.

PILCHARD SALAD

4 pilchards
8 oz. apples, cubed (may be
  omitted if not available)
8 oz. cold cooked potatoes, cubed
2 tablespoons chopped parsley
1 tablespoon chopped leek
  or onion

2 tablespoons salad dressing
8 oz. finely shredded cabbage
  or other greens
Watercress
1 dozen radishes

METHOD

Flake the fish and mix with the apples (if used), potatoes, 1 tablespoon parsley, leek or onion and salad dressing. Arrange the shredded greens on a dish, pile the fish mixture on top and decorate with the remaining parsley, watercress and radishes.

Raw Vegetable Salad

*10 tablespoons grated
raw carrot*
*8 tablespoons grated
raw turnip*
*4 tablespoons grated
raw parsnip*
*2 tablespoons finely
chopped onion*

*2 tablespoons finely
chopped celery*
*3 tablespoons coarsely
chopped watercress*
2 tablespoons salad dressing
Sprigs of watercress to decorate

METHOD

Mix vegetables together and moisten with the salad dressing. Turn into a salad bowl, decorate with sprigs of watercress.

Potato Salad

1½ lb. potatoes
¼ pint salad dressing

1 tablespoon chopped chives
1 tablespoon chopped mint

METHOD

Scrub potatoes and boil until tender. Peel while still warm and cut into large dice. Mix with salad dressing and herbs and place in salad bowl. Serve cold.

Mixed Vegetable Salad

1 cup cooked peas (fresh or dried)
1 cup cooked chopped beetroot
1 cup grated carrot
½ cup grated turnip

1½ cups shredded cabbage
*1 tablespoon coarsely
chopped fresh herbs*

METHOD

The vegetables can be arranged in strips on an oval dish, for example, cabbage, beetroot, turnip, carrot, peas, or mixed together in a bowl with salad dressing. Garnish with mixed herbs, for example, nasturtium leaves, parsley, mint, dandelion leaves, or watercress.

CABBAGE AND FRUIT SALAD

3 cups finely shredded cabbage
1 cup chopped apple
¹/₂ cup chopped ripe pear
1 tablespoon finely
   chopped onion
¹/₂ cup grated carrot
1 dessertspoon chopped mint
3-4 tablespoons salad dressing
Salt and pepper

METHOD

Mix together the cabbage, apple, pear, onion, carrot and mint. Moisten with the salad dressing and add a little salt and pepper if necessary. Pile on to dish and garnish with small sprigs of mint.

CELERY, BEETROOT AND BLANCHED CABBAGE

1¹/₂ lb. cabbage
1 pint boiling water
1 cup shredded beetroot

1 cup finely sliced celery
1 tablespoon chopped onion or leek
Salt and pepper

METHOD

Shred the cabbage, add to the boiling water and boil for 2 minutes. Drain and arrange round a dish forming a border. Mix together the beetroot, celery and onion or leek, seasoning well. Pile in the centre of the dish and serve with dressing handed separately.

FISH SALAD

1 cup chopped spinach
1½ cups grated carrot
1 cup sliced cauliflower

4 pilchards
Salad dressing
A few sprigs of cauliflower

METHOD

Mix spinach, carrot and cauliflower together and place in bowl. Lay fish on top and decorate with salad dressing and sprigs of cauliflower.

NOTE: Soused herrings, mackerel or sardines may be used instead of pilchards.

EGG AND CABBAGE SALAD

4 hard-boiled eggs
4 cups finely shredded cabbage
1 cup chopped watercress

¼ pint salad dressing
1 large tomato
¼ cup chopped cooked beetroot

METHOD

Chop up the eggs into small dice and mix with cabbage, watercress and salad dressing. Place in salad bowl and decorate with the remaining egg, tomato and beetroot.

HORS D'OEUVRE SALAD (ONE PORTION)

1 dried egg (scrambled)
1 teaspoon chopped herbs
2-3 lettuce leaves
2 tablespoons chopped
*   cooked beetroot*

1 sardine
Radish rose
2 tablespoons raw grated turnip
3 tablespoons cooked beans
2 tablespoons grated cheese

METHOD

The scrambled egg is mixed with the herbs and placed on the lettuce leaves. The other ingredients are arranged in heaps round this.

NOTE: This may also be served in an hors d'oeuvres dish. Other cooked or raw vegetables, mixed pickles and tomato roses may be used as alternatives in the above recipe.

SAUSAGE AND POTATO SALAD

1-1½ lb. cooked diced potatoes
4 cold boiled sausages
2-3 tablespoons chopped pickle
Salad dressing to moisten
*   (about 4 tablespoons)*

½ cup cooked peas
¼ cup cooked diced beetroot
12-16 radishes

METHOD

Mix potatoes, sausages and chopped pickle with salad dressing. Place in salad bowl and decorate with peas, beetroot and radishes.

Various Salad Dressings

Thin salad dressing (for use in place of oil and vinegar dressing).

½ teaspoon mustard   Pinch of pepper
½ teaspoon salt   2 tablespoons top of milk
½ teaspoon sugar   1 tablespoon vinegar

METHOD

Mix the seasoning together and mix in the milk gradually. When quite smooth, add the vinegar and stir well. Use the same day.

Economical Salad Dressing

2 oz. flour   ¼ teaspoon pepper
1 tablespoon sugar   1 pint milk or milk
2 teaspoons mustard   and vegetable water
2 teaspoons salt   4 tablespoons vinegar

METHOD

Mix dry ingredients together and blend with a little milk. Boil the rest of the milk and pour on to blended flour. Return to saucepan, stir until boiling and boil for 5 minutes. Whisk in vinegar.

CREAMY SALAD DRESSING

2 tablespoons flour
1 tablespoon dried egg
1 teaspoon mustard
1 teaspoon sugar
1 teaspoon salt

Pepper
½ pint milk or vegetable water
1 oz. margarine
4 tablespoons vinegar

METHOD

Mix the flour, dried egg, mustard, sugar, salt and pepper. Mix to a smooth paste with a little of the milk or vegetable water. Boil remaining liquid, pour on to the blended flour, return to pan and bring to the boil. Boil 5 minutes stirring well. Remove from heat and add margarine. Mix well and add vinegar.

Supper Dishes

CHEESE PANCAKE

4 oz. flour
2 oz. cooked mashed potato
2 oz. grated cheese
1½ gills (a gill equals ¼ pint)
   of milk and water

1 teaspoon baking powder
Salt and pepper
Pinch of mixed herbs

METHOD

Mix the flour, mashed potato and liquid to make a batter, add baking powder and cheese. Melt fat in a frying pan and when smoking hot pour in sufficient batter to cover the bottom of the pan. Fry pancakes to golden brown on each side. If liked, this mixture can be made into drop scones, using a greased hotplate or frying pan.

VEGETABLE AU GRATIN

*3 breakfast cups diced
   cooked vegetables*
*1 breakfast cup cooked white
   or coloured beans*
1 small piece chopped leek
3 oz. grated cheese

For the sauce:
4 oz. flour
½ pint vegetable liquid
½ pint milk

METHOD

Mix the flour to a smooth paste with some of the liquid. Bring the rest of the liquid to the boil and pour over blended flour. Return quickly to the pan and cook for 5 minutes, stirring all the time. Add cooked vegetables and half the cheese. Pour into a fireproof dish. Sprinkle with remainder of the cheese. Grill until brown, or brown at the top of the oven if the oven is in use.

CHEESE FRIZZLES

*4 tablespoons medium
   or coarse oatmeal*
2 tablespoons flour
4 tablespoons grated cheese

2 teaspoons baking powder
Salt and pepper
A little water to mix
Fat for frying

METHOD

Mix all dry ingredients together except the baking powder. Add enough cold water to mix to a stiff batter. Just before using add the baking powder. Melt a little fat in a frying pan and when smoking hot drop spoonfuls of the mixture into hot fat. Fry till golden brown on both sides.

CHEESE PUDDING

2 dried eggs (reconstituted)   1 teacupful breadcrumbs
½ pint milk   Salt and pepper
2-3 oz. grated cheese   Mustard

METHOD

Beat the eggs. Boil the milk, stir in the breadcrumbs and remove from the heat. Add cheese, salt, pepper, mustard and beaten eggs. Pour into a dish and bake or grill till brown.

CHEESE FONDANT SANDWICHES

4 oz. cheese, finely grated   1 teaspoon chopped
1 tablespoon dried milk   pickle or chutney
1 tablespoon water   Seasoning:
2 tablespoons coarsely   Few drops of
    chopped parsley   Worcester sauce if liked

METHOD

Blend all ingredients together and season well. The mixture should be quite soft.

Desserts, Puddings, Cakes, Biscuits and Scones

MADEIRA CAKE

2 dried eggs (reconstituted or fresh)   2 level teaspoons baking powder
½ lb. national flour   A little milk
2½ oz. margarine   Flavouring if liked
3 oz. sugar

METHOD

Beat eggs. Cream margarine and sugar, add eggs one by one, beating thoroughly. Add flour, baking powder and flavouring. Bake in a moderate oven for 1½-2 hours.

CAKE OR PUDDING MIXTURE

1 dried egg	*2 oz. fat*
(reconstituted or used dry)	*1 level teaspoon baking powder*
4 oz. flour	*A little milk*
2 oz. sugar	

METHOD

Beat egg. Cream fat and sugar, beat in egg, add the flour mixed with the baking powder. Mix to a soft consistency with a little milk. Spread in tin and bake for 15-20 minutes.

NOTE: This mixture can be steamed in a basin for 1 hour and served as a pudding with a jam or custard sauce.

COQUET PUDDING

½ lb. potatoes	*¼ pint household milk*
1½ oz. margarine	*1 tablespoon dried fruit*
1½ oz. sugar	*or 1 tablespoon jam*
2 eggs (reconstituted or used dry)	

METHOD

Cook and mash potatoes with margarine. Add sugar and eggs, beating well. Mix in milk and fruit and pour into a greased pie dish. Bake in a moderate oven for 30 minutes.

YORKSHIRE PUDDING

1 dried egg
 (reconstituted or used dry)
4 oz. national flour

Salt
1 knob dripping or fat
½ pint milk

METHOD

Beat egg well. Mix flour and salt. Make a hole in the centre and put in the egg and sufficient milk to make a stiff mixture. Beat well, add the rest of the milk. Melt fat in a baking tin and when smoking hot pour in the batter. Cook in a brisk oven for about 30 minutes.

NOTE: To this foundation recipe, diced cooked vegetables and chopped cooked meat can be added. The addition of fresh or dried fruit makes an attractive sweet dish. The same mixture can be used for pancakes. Pour spoonfuls on to a piping hot greased pan or hotplate.

Desserts

STEAMED CUSTARD (TWO PORTIONS)

2 dried eggs (reconstituted)
½ pint milk

Sugar
Flavouring

METHOD

Beat eggs, and sugar, add milk and flavouring, pour into a greased cup or mould, steam in a saucepan until set.

BAKED CUSTARD (TWO PORTIONS)

1½ dried eggs (reconstituted) *Sugar*
½ pint milk *Flavouring*

METHOD

Beat egg and sugar, add milk and flavouring, pour into a greased dish and bake till set in a slow oven.

NOTE: This can be baked in a pastry case and served as a custard flan.

STEAMED PUDDING WITH JAM

6 oz. plain flour and *1½ oz. sugar*
3 teaspoons baking powder *Just over 1 pint milk*
or 6 oz. self-raising flour *and water*
Pinch of salt *2 tablespoons jam*
1½ oz. margarine
or cooking fat

METHOD

Mix together the flour, baking powder if used, and salt. Rub in the margarine or fat and add the sugar. Mix to a dropping consistency with milk and water. Put the jam at the bottom of a greased tin and add the pudding mixture. Cover with lid and steam for 1½-2 hours.

MOCHA WHIP

8 tablespoons flour *1 tablespoon cocoa*
3 oz. sugar *1 pint black coffee*

METHOD

Mix the dry ingredients to a smooth paste with a little of the liquid. Bring the remainder to the boil and pour on to the blended mixture. Return to the pan and stir until it boils. Boil gently for 5 minutes, stirring frequently. Leave to cool, then whisk until light and frothy. Serve in 4 individual glasses.

SUMMER PUDDING

8 oz. fresh fruit
  (red or black if possible)
1-2 oz. sugar

¼ pint water
5 oz. stale bread,
  cut ¼" to ½" thick

METHOD

Stew the fruit with the sugar and water until tender. Cut a round of bread to fit the bottom of a basin (1 pint size) and line the side with fingers of bread, cut slightly wider at one end than the other. Fit the fingers of bread together so that no basin shows through. Half fill the basin with stewed fruit. Cover with a layer of scraps of bread left from cutting the round, etc. Add the remaining fruit and cover with a layer of bread. Pour the rest of the juice over all and cover the pudding with a weighted plate or saucer. Leave for at least two hours to cool and set. Turn out carefully and serve with custard.

NOTE: Very juicy fruit does not require any water for stewing. Bottled fruit may be used if fresh fruit is not available.

SEMOLINA MOULD

Semolina consists of the large hard grains of wheat left after flour has been bolted, and was much used during wartime rationing as the base for puddings, soups, etc.

4 tablespoons semolina
2 tablespoons sugar
Pinch of salt

1 pint milk or fruit juice
Flavouring to taste

METHOD

Mix the semolina, sugar, and salt to a smooth paste with a little of the cold liquid. Boil the remaining liquid and, when boiling, pour it on the blended semolina. Mix well, return to the pan, stir until it boils and boil for 5 minutes. Flavour to taste and pour into a wetted mould. Leave to set. Serve with jam.

STEAMED CHOCOLATE PUDDING

5 oz. self-raising flour
  or 5 oz. plain flour and
  2½ teaspoons baking powder
1 tablespoon sugar

2 tablespoons cocoa
1 oz. margarine or cooking fat
2 tablespoons syrup
6 tablespoons milk and water

METHOD

Mix the dry ingredients thoroughly and rub in the margarine or fat. Slightly warm the syrup and milk and water and add to the dry ingredients, beating until the consistency of batter. Pour into 4 small greased moulds or cups, cover with greased paper and steam for ½-¾ hour.

SWISS ROLY POLY

6 oz. prepared rhubarb,
  or any fresh fruit, chopped
2 tablespoons mixed dried fruit
Pinch of mixed spice

2 tablespoons breadcrumbs
1 tablespoon any red jam
6 oz. pastry

METHOD

Mix together the rhubarb, dried fruit, spice, breadcrumbs and jam for the filling. Roll the pastry to an oblong, spread with the filling and damp the edges. Roll up like a Swiss roll and seal the ends. Place on a greased tin, brush with milk and bake in a moderate oven for 30-40 minutes.

SUET CRUST PUDDING (I)

6 oz. plain flour
2 teaspoons baking powder
1 teaspoon salt
1-½ lb. suet or cooking fat
1 oz. grated raw potato

Water to mix
 (about 4 tablespoons)
1 lb. fresh fruit
1½-2 oz. sugar

METHOD

Mix the flour, baking powder and salt together. Add the suet, or rub in the fat, and potato and mix to a soft dough with water. Roll out two thirds of the dough and line a one-pint basin. Fill with fruit and sugar and moisten the edges of the lining. Roll the remaining dough to the size of the top of the basin and cover the fruit. Press the edges of dough together, cover with greased paper and steam for 1¼ hours.

BREAD AND BUTTER PUDDING

3-4 thin slices of lightly
 buttered bread
⅓ cup currants or sultanas
 (golden raisins)
1 tablespoon caster sugar
 (superfine granulated)

¾ pint milk
2 dried eggs (reconstituted or fresh)
Ground nutmeg

METHOD

Cut the buttered bread and butter into strips about ½" wide and arrange these, buttered side up, in layers in a greased ovenproof dish, sprinkling each layer with fruit and sugar. Heat the milk without allowing it to come to the boil. Whisk the eggs lightly, pour the milk on them, stirring all the time. Strain the mixture over the bread. Sprinkle a little bit of ground nutmeg on top and let the mixture stand for ¼ hour. Bake in a moderate oven for 30-40 minutes or until set and lightly browned.

DUMPLINGS WITH SYRUP

4 oz. plain flour and   *Pinch of salt*
  2 teaspoons baking powder   *1 oz. suet*
  or 4 oz. self-raising flour   *Water to mix*

METHOD

Mix all the dry ingredients together and add enough water to make a soft dough. Divide into 8 portions and roll into dumplings. Cook in boiling water for 10-15 minutes. Strain and serve with syrup.

Steamed Puddings

PLAIN STEAMED PUDDING

8 oz. plain flour   *2 oz. sugar*
Pinch of salt   *Milk, or milk and water to mix*
4 level teaspoons baking powder   *(just over ¼ pint)*
2 oz. fat   *2 dried eggs*

METHOD

Mix together flour, salt, baking powder and dried eggs. Rub in the fat until the mixture resembles breadcrumbs. Add sugar, and enough liquid to make the mixture a dropping consistency. Turn into a greased 6" basin and steam for 1 hour.

VARIATIONS OF PLAIN STEAMED PUDDING, DIRECTLY ABOVE

Fruit Pudding

Plain steamed pudding, with 2-3 oz. dried fruit added with the sugar.

Spice Pudding

Plain steamed pudding, with 2-3 oz. dried fruit and 2 level teaspoons mixed spice added with the sugar.

Chocolate Pudding

Plain steamed pudding, with 3 level tablespoons cocoa added with the sugar and ½-1 oz. sugar, or syrup added with the liquid.

Jam or Marmalade Pudding

Put 2 tablespoons of jam or marmalade in the bottom of the basin.

SUET CRUST PUDDING (II)

8 oz. plain flour
Pinch of salt
2 level teaspoons baking powder
1 oz. grated suet, or other fat
1 oz. grated raw potato
Water to mix (about 4 tablespoons)

METHOD

Mix together the flour, salt and baking powder. Add the suet (if other fat is used, rub this into the flour, etc., until the mixture resembles breadcrumbs), grated potato and enough water to mix to a stiff consistency. Roll out ¾ of the mixture, line a greased 7" basin with this. Fill the basin with fruit and sugar (approximately ½ lb. fruit plus 2-3 oz. sugar), moisten the edge of the pastry with water. Roll out the remaining ¼ of pastry and cover the contents of the basin with this. Press the edges well together. Steam for 1-1½ hours.

POTTER PUDDING

2½ oz. margarine
3 oz. sugar
2 dried eggs
4 tablespoons water
Flavouring essence
6 oz. plain flour

4 level teaspoons
   baking powder
3 oz. breadcrumbs
A little milk
2 oz. raisins, or ½ lb. apples,
   or 2 oz. jam or marmalade

METHOD

Cream the margarine and sugar with the dried eggs, adding the water gradually during creaming. Add essence, sift the flour and baking powder and add to the creamed mixture. Add the breadcrumbs and sufficient milk to make a soft consistency. Grease a pudding basin and place the raisins or jam, or peeled and sliced apples in the bottom. Add the pudding mixture and cover with greased paper. Steam for 1½ hours.

JACK HORNER PUDDING

6 oz. plain flour
2 level teaspoons baking powder
½ teaspoon salt
1½ oz. suet or fat
1½ oz. grated raw potato

Water to mix
1 lb. fresh fruit or
   6 oz. dried apricots or
   apple, soaked overnight
Sugar to sweeten or saccharin

METHOD

Mix flour, baking powder and salt. Rub in fat or add suet. Add potato. Mix to a stiff dough with water. Roll out ½" thick and the size of a saucepan top. Put fruit into pan with the sugar and a little water if fresh fruit is used or cover with water if dried fruit is used. When boiling, put in the pastry round and cook about 30-45 minutes, dish up with fruit piled on pastry.

EQUALITY PUDDING

2 oz. cooking fat or margarine
8 oz. plain flour
1½-2 tablespoons sugar

2 tablespoons jam
1 teaspoon bicarbonate of soda
Approx. ¼ pint milk and water

METHOD

Rub the cooking fat or margarine into the flour and mix in the sugar. Add the jam, dissolve the bicarbonate of soda in a little milk and mix the pudding to a soft dropping consistency. Turn into a greased basin, 1½ pint size, and steam for 2 hours. Serve with custard or a sweet sauce.

JAM SAUCE

1 tablespoon jam
¼ pint water

1 teaspoon cornflour or custard
powder or 2 teaspoons flour

METHOD

Put the jam and water in a small pan and bring to the boil. Blend the cornflour, custard powder or flour with a little cold water (about 2 teaspoons), pour the boiling liquid on to this. Return to the pan and boil gently for 5 minutes, stirring carefully. Serve with steamed puddings.

Baked Puddings

APPLE CHARLOTTE

1 lb. apples, or other fruit
6 oz. breadcrumbs
2-3 oz. sugar

½ level teaspoon cinnamon,
nutmeg or mixed spice
2 oz. margarine, melted

METHOD

Prepare the fruit, and cut it into thin slices. Mix together the breadcrumbs, sugar, spice and melted margarine. Arrange a layer of the breadcrumb mixture in a greased pint-size pie dish, then a layer of fruit, and continue filling the pie dish with alternate layers of breadcrumbs and fruit until all the ingredients are used up, finishing with a layer of the breadcrumb mixture. Bake in a moderate oven for ¾-1 hour. Serve hot.

VARIATIONS OF APPLE CHARLOTTE RECIPE ABOVE

Prune Pudding

Replace apples with ¼ lb. prunes, soaked, stoned and cut into pieces.

Chocolate Apple Charlotte

Add 2 level tablespoons cocoa to the breadcrumbs.

Apple Marmalade Charlotte

Add 4-6 level tablespoons marmalade to the breadcrumb mixture to replace the sugar.

COTTAGE PUDDING

8 oz. plain flour	*1 dried egg*
Pinch salt	*3 oz. sugar*
4 level teaspoons baking powder	*Milk to mix (about ¼ pint)*
3 oz. fat	

METHOD

Mix together the flour, salt and baking powder. Rub the fat into this mixture. Add the dried egg, sugar and enough milk to make the mixture to a soft consistency. Turn the mixture into a greased Yorkshire pudding tin, and bake in a moderate oven for 30-40 minutes. Cut into squares and serve with custard or other sauce.

VARIATIONS OF COTTAGE PUDDING RECIPE ABOVE

Eve's Pudding

2 lb. apples or 1-2 lb. other fruit prepared and put into a pie dish and covered with the cottage pudding mixture.

Ginger Cottage Pudding

Cottage pudding, with 3-4 level teaspoons ginger added with sugar.

NOTE: Some of the sugar in the cottage pudding recipe may be replaced by syrup in the Ginger Cottage Pudding.

BREAD AND MARMALADE PUDDING

4 oz. breadcrumbs	*1 pint milk, fresh or household*
3-4 tablespoons marmalade	

METHOD

Place half the breadcrumbs in a 1½ pint pie dish. Spread over the marmalade and cover with the remaining breadcrumbs, adding the milk last. Bake in a moderate oven for 1-½ hours, when the pudding should be set and golden brown.

Milk Puddings

SEMOLINA PUDDING

4 *level tablespoons semolina*
1 *level tablespoon sugar*
1 *pint milk, fresh,*
   household or tinned

Grated nutmeg
Pinch of salt

METHOD

Mix the semolina, sugar and salt with a little of the cold liquid. Boil the remaining liquid and, when boiling, pour it into the blended semolina. Mix well, return to the pan, stir until it boils and boil 5 minutes or cook 15 minutes over hot water. Pour the mixture into a pie dish and grate a little nutmeg on top. Bake in a moderate oven for about ½ hour till brown on top.

AMERICAN BREAD PUDDING

3-4 *oz. bread, cut in*
   small cubes (including crusts)
1 *pint milk*
½ *oz. margarine*
1 *tablespoon sugar*

1 *dried egg (reconstituted)*
Pinch of salt
1 *teaspoon vanilla*
   or ¼ teaspoon spice

METHOD

Heat the milk and margarine and pour on the bread. Set aside to cool. Add remaining ingredients, mix well and bake until set in a moderate oven.

VARIATIONS OF THE ABOVE

Spread top with jam or marmalade before serving, or add a little dried fruit before baking, or add 2 tablespoons cocoa and an extra tablespoon sugar.

Cold Sweets

CORNFLOUR MOULD

1½ to 2 oz. cornflour,   *Pinch of salt*
    custard powder, or arrowroot   *1 pint milk*
1½ oz. sugar   *Flavouring*

METHOD

Mix the cornflour, sugar and salt to a smooth paste with a little milk. Boil the rest of the milk, and add this slowly to the blended cornflour. Return the mixture to the pan, add the flavouring, bring to the boil, and stirring well all the time, boil the mixture 5 minutes or longer. Pour the mixture into a wetted mould, and leave till cold, and set before turning out.

VARIATIONS OF CORNFLOUR MOULD RECIPE ABOVE

Chocolate Mould

Cornflour Mould recipe with the addition of 2 level tablespoons cocoa added with the cornflour, sugar, etc.

Coffee Mould

Cornflour Mould recipe using ½ pint milk and ½ pint strong black coffee to make up the pint of liquid.

NOTE: The Coffee Mould may be found too sweet by some. If this is the case the sugar could be cut down to 1 oz.

MEXICAN CREAM

2 level tablespoons
  dried egg
2 level tablespoons flour
2-4 level tablespoons cocoa
2-4 level tablespoons sugar

Pinch of salt
1 pint moderately
  strong coffee
Vanilla essence

METHOD

Mix the dry ingredients together and mix to a smooth paste with a little coffee. Boil the remaining coffee. Pour on to the other ingredients, return to the pan and boil 5 minutes. Add vanilla essence and pour into individual glasses or a serving dish. Serve cold.

FRUIT CREAMS

½ lb. fruit
½ pint milk
Colouring, if necessary

2 level dessertspoons semolina
Sugar to taste

METHOD

Stew the fruit in as little water as possible. Boil the milk, sprinkle on the semolina. Stir until the mixture thickens. Allow to cook for 15 minutes. Add the stewed fruit to the semolina, gradually, whisking all the time. Beat well for 2-3 minutes. Add the sugar and suitable colouring. Serve cold.

Betty Brown (also known as Brown Betty)

3 oz. unsalted butter
1 cooking apple, peeled
  and cut into ¹/₂" slices
4 oz. white breadcrumbs

3 tablespoons soft brown sugar
1 teaspoon ground cinnamon
Icing sugar, to dust

METHOD

Gently melt 2 oz. of the butter in a large pan and sauté the apple slices for 4-5 minutes or until soft. Melt the remaining butter in a separate pan and fry the breadcrumbs, sugar and cinnamon for 3-4 minutes. Place half the apples in a layer on the base of an ovenproof dish, then top with the breadcrumb mixture. Repeat this process, finishing with a layer of breadcrumbs. Bake in a warm oven for 10-12 minutes or until golden. Sprinkle with icing sugar before serving.

Cakes, Biscuits and Scones without Eggs

The egg ration, whether provided as fresh eggs or in dried form, was severely limited in wartime, so a great deal of ingenuity went into creating recipes that closely imitated more traditional ones but which did not require any eggs.

Eggless Plain Cake

(This also serves as the 'foundation recipe' referred to in various recipes that follow immediately.)

½ lb. plain flour and	3 oz. margarine
4 teaspoons baking powder	3 oz. sugar
or ½ lb. self-raising flour	1 teaspoon vanilla essence
Pinch of salt	Approx. ½ pint milk and water

METHOD

Mix flour, baking powder, margarine if used, and add the sugar mixing to a dropping consistency with the milk and water. Turn into a greased 7" tin and bake in a moderate oven for ¾-1 hour.

VARIATIONS OF THE FOUNDATION RECIPE ABOVE

Rock Buns Variation

Foundation recipe with the addition of 4 oz. dried fruit and ½ teaspoon mixed spice, added with the sugar. Use as little liquid as possible for mixing so that the mixture is very stiff and will stand up in small heaps on a greased baking sheet. Bake in a hot oven for 10-15 minutes.

Plain Fruit Cake

Use the Rock Buns recipe directly above, but make the mixture to a dropping consistency and turn into a greased 7" tin and bake in a moderate oven for ¾-1 hour.

Ginger Cake

Use the foundation recipe and add 2 teaspoons ground ginger and 1½ teaspoon mixed spice with the flour. Put in a 7" tin and bake in a moderate oven for ¾-1 hour.

Chocolate Cake

Use the foundation recipe and add 3 tablespoons cocoa with the sugar. Put in a 7" tin and bake in a moderate oven for ³/₄-1 hour.

Raspberry Buns

Foundation recipe, but 2 oz. instead of 3 oz. sugar and 1 tablespoon jam, raspberry if possible. Save 1 dessertspoon sugar for coating and use only enough milk to mix to a stiff dough which can be cut into 12 equal pieces. Form into buns and make a hole in the middle. Put in a little jam and pull the dough over to cover it. Roll in sugar and place on a greased baking sheet. Bake in a hot oven for 10 minutes.

FRUIT CAKE

2 oz. margarine	1 oz. sugar
or cooking fat	4 oz. chopped dates
½ lb. plain flour and	or other dried fruit
4 teaspoons baking powder	¾ pint milk and water
or ½ lb. self-raising flour	3 saccharin tablets
Pinch of salt	

METHOD

Rub the fat into the flour, baking powder if used, and salt. Add the sugar and dried fruit. Mix to a soft consistency with milk and water in which the saccharin tablets have been dissolved. Turn the mixture into a greased 6" tin and bake in a moderate oven for about 1 hour.

Bun Loaf

2 oz. margarine or lard
1/2 lb. plain flour
Pinch of salt
2 oz. sugar
1/2 teaspoon mixed spice

3 oz. chopped dried fruit
1/4 pint milk and water
1 tablespoon vinegar
1 teaspoon bicarbonate of soda

METHOD

Rub the margarine or lard into the flour and salt. Add the sugar, spice and dried fruit and mix well. Add the milk and water and vinegar and beat well. Lastly, mix in the bicarbonate of soda dissolved in a little warm water and turn the mixture into a greased 6" tin. Bake in a moderate oven for 3/4 hour.

Gingerbread Cake

1 lb. self-raising flour
6 oz. syrup
1 teaspoon ground ginger

1 teaspoon bicarbonate of soda
1/4 pint tepid water

METHOD

Place the flour and syrup in a basin. Mix the ginger and bicarbonate of soda with the tepid water, add to the flour and syrup and mix all together. Turn into a greased tin, about 11" x 7", and bake in a moderate oven for about 1¼ hours. Do not cut for 2 days.

QUEEN CAKES

2½ oz. margarine
2 oz. sugar
1 tablespoon syrup
6 oz. self-raising flour
    or 6 oz. plain flour and
    3 teaspoons baking powder

Few drops vanilla essence
Pinch of salt
¼ pint milk and water
1½ oz. currants

METHOD

Cream the margarine and sugar together until light, then add the syrup and vanilla essence and beat well again. Sieve the flour, baking powder if used, and salt and add to the creamed mixture with the milk and water. Add the currants, mix well and put into greased bun tins. Bake in a moderate oven for 20-25 minutes. This quantity makes approximately 1 dozen cakes.

CHOCOLATE CAKE

3 oz. margarine or fat
7 oz. plain flour
1 teaspoon baking powder
½ teaspoon salt
1½ oz. cocoa

3 oz. sugar
¼ pint warm milk and water
1 teaspoon bicarbonate of soda
1 tablespoon vinegar
½ teaspoon vanilla essence

METHOD

Rub the margarine or fat into the flour, baking powder and salt. Add the cocoa and sugar and mix with the milk and water. Dissolve the bicarbonate of soda in the vinegar and add to the cake mixture with the vanilla essence. Mix, turn into a greased 6" tin and bake in a moderate oven for 1½ hours.

CHOCOLATE SPONGE

½ lb. self-raising flour
¼ teaspoon salt
2 tablespoons cocoa
3 oz. sugar
1 tablespoon syrup

12-14 tablespoons hot water
1 teaspoon bicarbonate of soda
3 oz. margarine or lard
Vanilla essence

METHOD

Mix the flour, salt, cocoa together. Dissolve the syrup in the water and add the bicarbonate of soda. Melt the margarine or lard and mix all the ingredients together, including the vanilla essence, but do not beat the mixture, which should be very soft. Divide the mixture evenly into two 8" sandwich tins and bake in a moderate oven for 20 minutes. When cool, use jam or a chocolate or cream filling between the two layers.

DRIPPING CAKE

½ lb. self-raising flour
or ½ lb. plain flour and
4 teaspoons baking powder
¼ teaspoon salt
½ teaspoon mixed spice

2 oz. clarified dripping
3 oz. sugar
3 oz. currants or sultanas
¼ pint milk

METHOD

Sift the flour, baking powder, if used, salt and spice together. Rub in the dripping and add the sugar and fruit. Mix to a soft consistency with the milk and turn into a greased 6" cake tin. Bake in a moderate oven for 50 minutes.

NOTE: If hard mutton dripping is used, it may be slightly warmed to make it easier to rub in.

Biscuits

DIGESTIVE BISCUITS

2 oz. fat

6 oz. self-raising flour or

  6 oz. plain flour and

  3 teaspoons baking powder

3 oz. oatmeal

1 oz. sugar

Pinch of salt

About ¼ pint water

METHOD

Rub the fat into the dry ingredients. Add just enough water to bind the dough. Knead a little and roll out to less than ¼" thick. Cut into rounds. Place on a floured baking sheet and bake in a fairly cool oven until the biscuits are coloured. Makes 20-24 biscuits with a 3" cutter.

ANZAC BISCUITS

Named after the soldiers serving with the Australian and New Zealand Army Corps during World War I.

3 oz. margarine

3 oz. sugar

1 tablespoon syrup

½ teaspoon vanilla essence

1 teaspoon bicarbonate of soda

2 tablespoons hot water

3 oz. plain flour

½ lb. rolled oats

METHOD

Cream margarine and sugar. Add syrup and vanilla essence. Dissolve bicarbonate of soda in hot water and add flour and then oats to give a stiff consistency. Place teaspoons of the mixture on a tray 2" apart and cook in a moderate oven for 20 minutes. Makes 36 biscuits.

GINGER BISCUITS

2 oz. sugar

2 oz. syrup

2 oz. margarine or cooking fat

½ lb. plain flour

½ teaspoon mixed spice

2 teaspoons ginger

Lemon substitute

1 teaspoon bicarbonate of soda

1 tablespoon tepid water

METHOD

Melt in a pan the syrup, sugar and margarine or fat. Pour into a bowl. Add some flour and the spice, ginger and lemon substitute. Stir well. Dissolve the bicarbonate of soda in a tablespoon of tepid water, and add to mixture. Continue stirring, gradually adding more flour. Finish the process by turning out the mixture on to a well-floured board. Knead in the remainder of the flour. Roll out and cut into shapes. Cook in a moderate oven for 15-20 minutes. Makes approximately 24 biscuits.

SHORTBREAD

2 oz. margarine

3 oz. flour

1 oz. sugar

METHOD

Rub the margarine into the flour and sugar. Knead into a dough without adding any water. Roll out to about ½" and cut into biscuits. Bake in a cool oven until pale brown.

HONEY BISCUITS

2¹/₂ oz. margarine
6 oz. self-raising flour or
   6 oz. plain flour and
   3 teaspoons baking powder

1 oz. sugar
2 tablespoons honey
1 teaspoon cinnamon
Pinch of salt

METHOD

Cream the margarine and sugar. Add the honey, work in the flour, baking powder if used, cinnamon and salt. Roll out until `¹/₄" thick. Cut into rounds, place on a baking sheet, and bake in a moderate oven for 10 minutes. This quantity makes approximately 40-50 biscuits.

PEPPERMINT STICKS

1 lb. syrup
5 tablespoons water
Pinch cream of tartar or
   1 teaspoon vinegar

¹/₂ teaspoon peppermint
   essence or a few drops of
   oil of peppermint

METHOD

Bring the syrup and water to the boil slowly, and add the cream of tartar or vinegar. Boil until a little snaps when tested in cold water. Add the peppermint essence, and pour on to a greased plate. Leave till the edge takes the mark of the finger. Fold the sides of the mixture into the centre. Remove from the plate and pull the mixture until it becomes lighter in colour. Cut into 12 or 18 pieces, and pull into sticks. Leave to set on a flat greased surface.

CHOCOLATE CRUNCH

1 oz. margarine	*Pinch of salt*
4 tablespoons syrup	*4 oz. rolled oats or barley flakes*
1 tablespoon cocoa	

METHOD

Warm margarine and syrup and beat well. Add the cocoa and salt and beat again. Gradually work in the oats. Spread on a shallow greased tin (about 4"x6") and bake in a moderate oven for 20 minutes. Mark into fingers and cut when cold.

JAM BISCUITS

3 oz. fat	*2 tablespoons milk*
8 oz. flour	*3 tablespoons jam*

METHOD

Rub fat into the flour till the consistency of breadcrumbs. Mix together the milk and the jam. Add this to the fat and flour, knead well. Roll out very thinly, cut into shapes and bake in a moderate oven for 15 minutes.

Fillings for Cakes

CHOCOLATE FILLING

1 oz. margarine	*2 tablespoons strong black coffee*
2 oz. cocoa	*or 2 tablespoons water and*
2 oz. sugar	*1 teaspoon vanilla essence*

METHOD

Melt the margarine. Remove from the heat and add the cocoa and sugar Beat in the coffee, or water and vanilla essence, until mixture becomes of a good spreading consistency.

CREAM FILLINGS (2 VARIATIONS)

Variation 1

1 oz. margarine
1 oz. sugar
4 tablespoons household milk, dry

1 tablespoon warm water
Flavouring to taste

METHOD

Cream margarine and sugar till white and smooth. Add the milk and water gradually, beating well in till quite smooth. Add a few drops of flavouring to taste.

Variation 2

1 tablespoon custard powder
* or cornflour*
¼ pint milk

1 oz. margarine
½ oz. sugar
Flavouring

METHOD

Blend the custard powder or cornflour with a little cold milk. Warm the rest of the milk in a saucepan. Add it to the custard powder and return to the pan. Stir over heat till well cooked. Put aside to cool. Cream margarine and sugar together very well, beat in the thick custard, add flavouring, and continue to beat till creamy. This makes about ¼ pint of cream similar in texture to whipped cream.

Scones

PLAIN SCONES

½ lb. self-raising flour
  or ½ lb. plain flour and
  4 teaspoons baking powder

1 teaspoon salt
1 oz. margarine
¼ pint milk

METHOD

Mix the flour, baking powder if used, and salt together, rub in the margarine. Mix to a soft dough with milk. Turn on to a floured board and roll out to ¾" thickness. Cut into 8 rounds or triangles, put on a greased baking sheet and bake in a hot oven for 15 minutes. Serve hot or cold with a savoury or sweet sandwich filling.

SWEET SCONES

Use the Plain Scones recipe above but with 1 oz. sugar added after fat has been rubbed in. Proceed as before.

FRUIT SCONES

Plain Scones recipe above with the addition of 1 oz. sugar and 1 oz. dried fruit added after the fat has been rubbed in. Proceed as before.

GRIDDLE SCONES

(Also known as 'Girdle Scones', griddles once being known as 'girdles' in Northern England and Scotland.)

½ lb. plain flour and
  4 teaspoons baking powder
  or ½ lb. self-raising flour
½ teaspoon salt

½-1 oz. lard or cooking fat
Milk and water to mix
  (approx. ¼ pint)

METHOD

Mix the flour, baking powder if used, and salt. Rub in the fat and add enough milk and water to mix to a soft dough. Turn on to a floured board, knead lightly and roll out quickly to ¼" thick. Cut into triangles and place on a fairly hot griddle. Bake steadily until well risen and a light brown colour underneath; turn, and bake on the second side until cooked in the centre (the time required for cooking is from 10-15 minutes). This quantity makes about 14 scones, each 3"x2".

NOTE: An electric hotplate or thick frying pan may be used in place of a griddle.

Fruit-Based Recipes

To help the sugar ration stretch further, the Ministry of Food came up with several recipes that used dry fruit to add sweetness to biscuits, cakes, puddings, pies and sandwich fillings. Additionally, it recommended that stewing dried fruit with fresh fruit helped to save sugar as well as giving an interesting flavour.

FIG BISCUITS

For the pastry:
8 oz. plain flour
Pinch of salt
2 oz. cooking fat
Water to mix

For the filling:
2-3 oz. figs
4 tablespoons water
½ teaspoon ginger and mixed spice
Few drops lemon essence

METHOD

Mix the flour and salt and rub in the fat. Mix in water and work to a stiff dough. Chop up the figs and simmer in the water till quite soft. Add the spice, lemon essence, and allow to become quite cold. Roll pastry out into an oblong 12"x24" and ¼" thick. Spread half of the pastry with the filling, cover with the other half, bake in a hot oven for 10 minutes and cut into squares when cold. This quantity makes approximately 40 biscuits.

ALTERNATIVE DATE FILLING FOR USE WITH
BISCUIT PASTRY ABOVE

4 oz. dates
4 tablespoons water
2 teaspoons custard powder

1 teaspoon lemon essence
6 oz. short crust pastry

METHOD

Stone the dates and stew in the water until soft. Mix the custard powder to a smooth paste with a little cold water. Add it to the dates with the lemon essence. Bring to the boil and cook for 2-3 minutes stirring the whole time. Press the dates on the side of the pan to help to break them down. Line a 7" tin with the pastry and spread over the filling. Bake in a hot oven for 20-30 minutes.

DRIED FRUIT FRITTERS

4 oz. plain flour and
*   2 teaspoons baking powder*
*   or 4 oz. self-raising flour*
Pinch of salt

¼ pint water
2 oz. any dried fruit, chopped
Fat for frying

METHOD

Mix the flour, baking powder if used, and salt to a batter with the water, add the fruit. Fry tablespoon of the mixture in hot fat until brown on both sides. Serve with a little sugar sprinkled over or with some melted syrup.

DATE FINGERS

2 oz. margarine

2 oz. syrup

3 oz. chopped dates

4 oz. barley kernels or
   flakes or rolled oats

1 teaspoon almond essence

2 oz. sell-raising flour or

   2 oz. plain flour and

1 teaspoon baking powder

METHOD

Melt the margarine and syrup over gentle heat. Stir in the dates and almond essence. Mix the barley kernels or flakes or rolled oats with the flour and baking powder if used, and stir into the ingredients in the pan. Spread out on a greased tin, pressing with damp fingers until the mixture is pressed down smoothly and about ½" in thickness. Bake in a moderate oven for 20-25 minutes. Leave for a few minutes to set and, while still warm, cut into fingers. Remove from the tin when cold.

MAKING THE MOST OF SUGAR

Sugar, of course, was in very short supply during the war years, and that was why the Ministry of Food created a wide variety of recipes for cakes and other desserts that either used very little sugar or even none. Naturally, these recipes are likely to be of particular interest today to anyone who wants to shed a few pounds by decreasing their calorie intake.

First, some advice on how to use saccharin:

For general sweetening, 3-4 standard tablets of saccharin are equal to 1 oz. of sugar. However, in many instances, the somewhat distinctive taste of saccharin will be considerably less noticeable if the saccharin is mixed with sugar to make what was called 'fortified sugar'.

Here is how you make and use that mixture:

Crush 30 standard saccharin tablets, using a rolling pin, and mix with 8 oz. sugar. This mixture will then equal 1 lb. of sugar in sweetness. It may be stored in a covered jar and used as required. When using this 'fortified sugar' only half the usual amount of sugar will be needed. For example, if a recipe normally requires 2 oz. sugar only 1 oz. of the fortified sugar will be required to give the same sweetening and if you generally have 1 teaspoon of sugar in tea or coffee only ½ a teaspoon of fortified sugar will be needed.

Saccharin or fortified sugar may be used for bottling fruit. It should be dissolved in water in the same way as when making a sugar syrup for bottling.

As far as sweetening custard, sauces and stewed fruit is concerned, when saccharin only is used, crush the tablets and stir in when cooking is finished. Better results are obtained by using the fortified sugar that can be added during cooking in the usual way.

NOTE: Saccharin should not be used in making jam, will not keep unless it contains the full amount of sugar.

PLAIN CAKE

3 oz. margarine
8 oz. plain flour and
    4 teaspoons baking powder
    or 8 oz. self-raising flour

2 oz. sugar and 7½ saccharin
    tablets (crushed)
Milk to mix (about ¼ pint)
Flavouring to taste

METHOD

Rub the margarine into the flour, add the baking powder if used, and sugar. Dissolve the saccharin tablets in a little warm milk and add to the mixture with more milk to form a soft consistency. Turn into a greased 7" diameter cake tin and cook for 1½-2 hours in a moderate oven.

ALTERNATIVE FLAVOURINGS FOR THE PLAIN CAKE RECIPE ABOVE

Ginger Cake

Add 2 teaspoons ground ginger and 1 teaspoon mixed spice with the flour.

Plain Fruit

Add 4 oz. dried fruit and ½ teaspoon mixed spice with the sugar.

Chocolate

Add 3 tablespoons cocoa with the sugar.

CHOCOLATE PEPPERMINT PIE

6 oz. short crust pastry	*1 oz. sugar*
4 tablespoons cornflour	*1 pint milk*
or 8 tablespoons flour	*4 saccharin tablets*
Pinch of salt	*Vanilla essence*
2 tablespoons cocoa	

METHOD

Line an 8" flan tin with the pastry and bake it blind in a hot oven. Mix the cornflour or flour, salt, cocoa and sugar with a little of the cold milk. Boil the rest of the milk and dissolve the saccharin tablets in it. Add slowly to the blended mixture and return to the pan. Bring to the boil stirring well and boil for 5 minutes stirring all the time. Add the vanilla essence and whisk well. Pour the mixture into the pastry case and when cool decorate with mock cream, flavoured with peppermint essence (see recipe directly below).

MOCK CREAM

(For use with the Chocolate Peppermint Pie above, but can also successfully accompany many other pie and cake recipes.)

1 oz. margarine	*1 tablespoon warm water*
1 oz. sugar	*Peppermint essence to taste*
1 tablespoon household milk, dry	

METHOD

Cream margarine and sugar till white and smooth. Add the milk and water gradually, beating well till quite smooth. Add a few drops of peppermint essence to taste.

SULTANA PUDDING

8 oz. plain flour and
    4 teaspoons baking powder
    or 8 oz. self-raising flour
Pinch of salt
1 tablespoon cocoa
1 teaspoon cinnamon
1 teaspoon spice

2 oz. cooking fat or suet
4 oz. sultanas
2 tablespoons syrup
½ teaspoon vanilla essence
6 saccharin tablets
About ¼ pint milk and
    water to mix

METHOD

Mix the flour, baking powder if used, salt, cocoa, cinnamon and spice. Rub in the fat or mix in the suet, add the sultanas. Add the syrup, vanilla essence and crushed saccharin tablets to the milk and water and use this to mix the pudding to a dropping consistency. Turn into a greased 2 pint-size basin and steam for 1½ hours.

SAVING SUGAR WITH SWEETENED CONDENSED MILK

Another ingenious approach to make the wartime sugar ration stretch further was to use sweetened condensed milk in recipes, as exemplified in the next two. Suggested the Ministry of Food: "Use condensed milk to save sugar in custards, sauces and all milk puddings. Dilute the milk according to the directions on the tin and then use as fresh milk."

CONDENSED MILK CAKE

3 oz. margarine
8 oz. self-raising flour or
   8 oz. plain flour and
   4 teaspoons baking powder
1 oz. sugar

3 oz. sultanas or raisins
1 tablespoon marmalade
3 tablespoons condensed milk made
   up to ¼ pint with water
2 beaten eggs, fresh or dried

METHOD

Rub the margarine into the flour and add the baking powder if used, sugar and dried fruit. Mix to a soft consistency with the marmalade, milk and beaten eggs. Turn into a greased 6" cake tin and bake in a moderate oven for 45 minutes.

CREAMY FRUIT WHIP

¾ pint thick fruit pulp or
   purée from bottled or fresh fruit

¼ pint sweetened condensed milk

METHOD

Mix the fruit pulp or purée with the condensed milk in a basin. Whisk for at least 10 minutes until light and frothing. Colour if necessary. Serve in individual glasses.

NOTE: A few drops of essence can be added for flavouring, for example, lemon essence with apples and almond essence with plums.

Cooking for One

Because cooking for only one person can all too easily become wasteful, the wartime Ministry of Food paid special attention to the needs of people living on their own, offering them a series of recipes that required relatively little effort to prepare while at the same time ensuring that there wouldn't be unnecessary leftovers. Both of these considerations remain equally valid today.

BREAKFAST DISHES

Savoury Potato Cakes (one portion)

2 tablespoons mashed potato

2 tablespoons cooked fish, flaked

1 teaspoon chopped parsley

½ teaspoon salt

Pinch of pepper

METHOD

Mix the ingredients well together. Turn on to a board and shape into 2 small cakes. Brown on both sides under the grill.

Alternative flavourings to use instead of fresh fish with Savoury Potato Cakes recipe above:

1)   1 tablespoon canned fish.

2)   2 tablespoons grated cheese.

3)   1½-2 tablespoons chopped cooked meat or sausage.

MEAT AND FISH MAIN MEALS FOR ONE

Cabbage and Mince Scramble

1½ dessertspoons fat (½ oz.)

2 cups shredded cabbage (6 oz.)

½ cup potatoes,
    thinly sliced (4 oz.)

2 teaspoons chopped leek
    or onion

3 tablespoons meat, minced
    or finely chopped (2 oz.)

½ teaspoon meat extract

2 tablespoons water

1 teaspoon salt

Pinch of pepper

METHOD

Make fat hot in a frying pan. Add cabbage, potatoes and leek or onion. Cook gently for 10 minutes, turning frequently without browning. Add meat, meat extract dissolved in the water and seasoning. Cover pan with plate or saucepan lid and simmer for 20-25 minutes. Stir to prevent sticking. Serve hot with a vegetable.

BRAISED LAMB CHOP

1 lamb chop	*2 or 3 peppercorns*
2 or 3 bacon rinds	*1 or 2 leaves mint*
¾ cup mixed	*½ teaspoon salt*
vegetables, diced	*Pinch of pepper*
1 tomato, if available	*½ cup stock or water*
1 clove	

METHOD

Trim all surplus fat from the chop. Heat the fat and the bacon rinds in a pan to extract the fat and fry the chop until well browned on both sides. Remove the chop and pour off the fat. Place the vegetables in the pan with the tomato, spices, seasoning and stock or water. Place the chop on the vegetables, cover the pan with a lid and boil very gently for ½-¾ hour. Remove the bacon rinds and serve the chop on a hot plate with the vegetables and gravy, which may be thickened with a little flour.

NOTE: Small joints such as breast of mutton, loin or topside may be cooked in this manner. A breast should be boned and a layer of stuffing spread over it; it is then rolled up and tied or skewered into position.

Any meat left over may be treated in the same way as meat from a cold roast.

CREAMED SALMON

1 tablespoon flour
½ teaspoon salt
Pinch of pepper
Pinch of mustard
4 tablespoons water

1 teaspoon vinegar
½ tin household salmon
  (¼ lb. size)
1 tablespoon chopped parsley

METHOD

Blend the flour and seasoning with the water and bring to the boil, stirring all the time. Boil gently for 3 minutes, then beat in the vinegar and salmon and cook over a low heat for 5 minutes. Add the parsley and serve hot on toast, or cold with salad

    NOTE: Use the remaining salmon to make a salad or fish pie or fish cakes.

VEGETABLES AND SALADS

INDIVIDUAL SALAD

4-5 tablespoons grated
  raw carrot
½ cup chopped or
  grated apple

2 tablespoons raisins or
  other dried fruit
3-4 curly lettuce leaves
1 tablespoon thick salad dressing

METHOD

Mix the carrot, apple and raisins together, keeping 2 or 3 raisins to garnish the top. Heap it in a nest of lettuce leaves. Garnish with salad dressing and raisins.

    The filling may be varied, using other fruit and vegetables such as pears, prunes, plums, swede, spinach, cucumber, celery and tomatoes.

Hors D'oeuvre Salad

2-3 sardines	*3 tablespoons cooked beans*
2-3 lettuce leaves	*3 tablespoons cooked*
3 tablespoons	*beetroot, chopped*
raw turnip, grated	*Finely grated cheese*

METHOD

Place the sardines on the lettuce leaves. Arrange the other ingredients in heaps around this and garnish with finely-grated cheese.

Coleslaw (one portion)

1 cup finely shredded	*1 small onion, chopped finely*
cabbage heart or sprouts	*½ tablespoon salad dressing*

METHOD

Mix the ingredients together and serve as an accompaniment to hot or cold meat or fish in place of a cooked vegetable.

SWEET DISHES FOR ONE

Steamed Pudding

6 tablespoons plain flour and	*Pinch of salt*
1 teaspoon baking powder or	*1 tablespoon sugar*
6 tablespoons self-raising flour	*Few drops of flavouring*
1 tablespoon margarine or	*3 tablespoons milk or*
cooking fat	*water to mix*

METHOD

Mix flour, baking powder if used, and salt. Rub in the margarine or fat and add the sugar. Mix with the flavouring and milk or water, turn into a greased ¼ pint basin, or 2 small moulds, and steam for 30-35 minutes. Serve with any sweet sauce. The remainder of the pudding may be eaten cold or reheated.

This recipe can be varied as follows:

1) **FRUIT PUDDING** – Add 2-3 tablespoons dried fruit with the sugar.

2) **CHOCOLATE PUDDING** – Add ½ tablespoon cocoa and ½ tablespoon sugar to the dry ingredients.

3) **GINGER OR SPICE PUDDING** – Add 1 teaspoon ground ginger or mixed spice to the dry ingredients.

4) **JAM PUDDING** – Place 1 tablespoon jam at the bottom of the basin before adding the pudding mixture.

FRUIT WHIP

1½ tablespoons semolina   *1 cup fruit juice or purée*
1 tablespoon sugar

METHOD

Blend semolina with a little of the fruit juice or purée. Bring the remainder to the boil. Pour on to the blended mixture and return to the pan. Stir over gentle heat, allow to boil for 7-10 minutes to cook the semolina. Sweeten to taste. Turn into a bowl and allow to cool. When cold, but not set, whisk thoroughly till light and fluffy. Serve cold.

ORANGE OR LEMON WHIP

1 tablespoon cornflour or   *2 tablespoons lemon or*
*   2 tablespoons plain flour*   *orange squash made up*
½ tablespoon sugar   *to ½ cup with water*

METHOD

Mix the dry ingredients to a smooth paste with a little of the liquid. Bring the remainder to the boil and pour on to the blended mixture. Return to the pan, bring to the boil and boil gently for 5 minutes, stirring frequently. Leave to cool, then whisk until light and frothy. Serve very cold.

SUPPER DISHES FOR ONE

FRENCH PEASANT SOUP (ONE PORTION)

1 cup mixed vegetables
(carrot, parsnips, potatoes, etc.)
1 cup boiling stock or water
1 teaspoon salt

2-3 tablespoons breadcrumbs
Pinch of pepper
2 tablespoons chopped parsley
½-1 oz. grated cheese

METHOD

Prepare and slice or dice the vegetables, place in the stock or water to which the salt has been added. Boil gently until tender, about 20 minutes. Add the breadcrumbs and simmer for a few minutes. Mash well, season and add the parsley and cheese just before serving.

SAUSAGE DUMPLINGS

6 tablespoons plain flour and
1 teaspoon baking powder or
6 tablespoons self-raising flour
2 tablespoons chopped cooked
sausage or liver or
breakfast sausage

Pinch of salt
Pinch of pepper
2 tablespoons milk to mix
¼ teaspoon meat or
vegetable extract
½ cup boiling water

METHOD

Mix the dry ingredients together, add the sausage and mix to a soft dough with milk or water. Form into 2 dumplings. Add the extract to the water and, when dissolved, add the dumplings. Boil for 15 minutes. Serve hot with the gravy.

PAN HASH (ONE PORTION)

½ rasher bacon, chopped
2 tablespoons mashed potato
2 tablespoons chopped
  cooked vegetables

½ teaspoon salt
Pinch of pepper
A little fat for frying,
  if necessary

METHOD

Fry the bacon until crisp, remove from the pan and mix with the potato, vegetables and seasoning. Fry the mixture in the bacon fat until well-browned for about 10 minutes.

NOTE: If no cooked vegetables are available, 4 tablespoons of mashed potato may be used.

Alternative flavourings you can use instead of bacon in this recipe:

1)   1 tablespoon chopped cooked meat; or

2)   1 tablespoon flaked cooked fish, or canned fish.

SAVOURY SPROUTS

½ lb. sprouts
1½ tablespoons flour
½ cup vegetable water
  and milk

3 tablespoons grated cheese
Few drops lemon essence
½ teaspoon salt
Pinch of pepper

METHOD

Prepare the sprouts and cook in a little boiling salted water until tender, drain and keep hot, saving the liquid. Blend the flour with a little of the liquid, bring the remainder to the boil and pour on to the blended flour. Return to the pan, bring to the boil, stirring all the time, and boil gently for 5 minutes. Add the cheese, a few drops of lemon essence and season well. Add the sprouts, reheat and serve very hot.

SARDINES AND CURRY SAUCE

½-1 teaspoon *curry powder*	*4 tablespoons water* *¼ teaspoon salt*
1-2 spring onions, *chopped finely*	*Few drops of vinegar* *½ can sardines*
1 teaspoon cooking fat *or dripping*	*(4½ oz. size)* *1 round of toast*
1 tablespoon flour	

METHOD

Fry the curry powder and onion in the fat for a few minutes. Work in the flour, add the water gradually and bring to the boil, stirring all the time. Boil gently for 5 minutes and add the salt and a few drops of vinegar. Place the sardines on the toast, pour over the curry sauce and serve at once.

NOTE: The remainder of the sardines can be used for sandwiches or in a salad.

BEVERAGES FOR ONE

COCOA

2½ tablespoons *household milk, dry*	*2-4 teaspoons cocoa* *½ pint water*
1 teaspoon sugar, or to taste	

METHOD

Mix the milk, sugar and cocoa to a smooth paste with a little of the water. Bring the remainder to the boil and add to the paste, stirring well. The flavour is greatly improved if the mixture is returned to the pan and allowed to boil for 1-2 minutes before serving.

BLACK COFFEE (TO MAKE 1 PINT)

2 tablespoons ground coffee   *1 pint freshly boiled water*

METHOD

Place the coffee grounds in a jug and leave in a warm place for 10 minutes, cover with boiling water, stir well and leave standing for 15-20 minutes. Pour off carefully without disturbing the grounds at the bottom of the jug. The coffee may need reheating before serving, but do not allow it to boil. Alternatively, stand the jug in boiling water while making the coffee.

WHITE COFFEE (MADE WITH VERY LITTLE MILK)

½ pint black coffee   *¼ pint water*
¼ pint milk (fresh or household)

METHOD

Make the black coffee according to the recipe directly above. Keep hot. Mix the milk and water together. Heat and serve in a jug.

BONUS SECTION

Traditional Cleaning Remedies and Tips

Just as the recipes of yesteryear have once again become relevant nowadays in that they can help alleviate many of the health problems associated with obesity and other diet-related disorders, there is also much to be said for exploring the numerous possibilities and distinct advantages offered by the many traditional household cleaning methods that were used in a bygone age.

While most of us have been virtually brainwashed through repetitive advertisements and TV commercials into using the modern 'wonder' offerings from the chemical industry, it is a fact that many of these 'latest' and seemingly endlessly 'improved' products are all too often not nearly as effective as the ones that were in common use some generations ago. What's more, almost invariably the traditional cleaning methods score better on several important points:

• They are invariably a good deal more inexpensive, usually costing mere pennies instead of pounds.

• They are also 'greener', creating the most limited impact, if any, on the environment. Additionally, their packaging is usually minimal, so making them ecologically sound by reducing waste and the need for landfill.

• They are very versatile, one simple old-fashioned cleaning remedy often being capable to tackling many different jobs that would otherwise require a dozen or so 'special' products that together would fill a cupboard shelf.

All of these are extremely good reasons why there is a good deal to be gained and precious little to be lost by trying out the various suggestions and tips that follow.

However, before going on to the tips themselves, let's first take a quick look at...

THREE TOP TRADITIONAL CLEANING AIDS

SODIUM BICARBONATE

This extremely useful chemical compound that can aid with all sorts of household tasks is known by many different names, including baking soda, bread soda, cooking soda, and bicarbonate of soda. However, no matter what it is called, its chemical formula is $NaHCO_3$, and it is a white crystalline compound that most often is presented as a fine powder. Found naturally in many mineral springs, sodium bicarbonate is also produced artificially.

Note that sodium bicarbonate is not quite the same as baking powder, as the latter also contains acidifying and drying agents, which when added to baked goods causes them to rise through the production of carbon dioxide bubbles that expand when exposed to oven temperatures.

As you'll see from the many tips that follow and feature it, sodium bicarbonate offers many advantages: it's extremely versatile, incredibly effective, and, of course, is truly super-cheap. What's more, it's also ecologically inoffensive.

VINEGAR

Another all-star old-fashioned cleaner is vinegar. Because it's mildly acidic, it really is a fantastic all-purpose dirt-removing agent that is extremely effective on solid stains, such as calcium deposits and limescale that all too often defeat even the best of commercial products. Additionally, vinegar has great sanitising properties, eradicating or substantially reducing the levels of a wide range of common household bacteria, moulds and yeasts. Another big plus is that it is totally biodegradable.

LEMON JUICE

Like vinegar, lemon juice is also acidic, containing citric acid, and therefore is extremely effective at dissolving almost any kind of grease, as well as having marked deodorising and bleaching effects. While you can buy bottled lemon juice, you'll usually get the best results by using juice obtained directly from the fruit. Hot tip: lemons that are firm and have fine-grained skins will generally yield the most juice.

IMPORTANT NOTE: Although all the tips listed below have been, as it were, 'road-tested' by generations of users, it still remains a sensible precaution to make sure that any given cleaning suggestion works well with whatever you're going to use it on by trying it first out on a small area that's usually hidden from sight. Following this recommendation is particularly important when you're not absolutely certain of the composition of whatever you intend to clean. For example, the apparent 'solid wood' finish of a piece of modern furniture could possibly not be wood at all, but instead be made of some synthetic plastic compound that could interact badly with, say, even the mild acidity of lemon juice.

AN ALPHABETICAL GUIDE TO TRADITIONAL AND NATURAL CLEANING AIDS

AIR FRESHENER

An extremely effective spray deodoriser is obtained by mixing 2 cups of clean water with 2 tablespoons of white vinegar and 1 teaspoon of sodium bicarbonate. Shake well after mixing and at various times while spraying.

ALABASTER

To clean ornaments and other items made from alabaster – a fine-grained, usually white, opaque, or translucent variety of gypsum used for statues, vases, etc. – first wash them with a warm solution of ordinary household soap and water. If there are stubborn stains, dampen a clean white cloth in turpentine, dip it into pumice powder and rub gently at them. Once the stains are gone, it is essential to remove every single trace of turpentine and pumice by thoroughly washing the object in lukewarm water in which a little borax was first dissolved.

ALUMINIUM

Never use metal cleaners or wire wool to clean the inside of saucepans, frying pans and similar utensils made of aluminium, because that harsh approach will expose a fresh layer of the surface which can then react with the food. It is particularly important to avoid this happening because there is considerable evidence linking aluminium cookware to the early onset of Alzheimer's. However, slight discoloration of the insides of aluminium cookware can be removed by filling the item with water, in which either half a lemon or some apple peelings have been placed and then bringing the mixture to the boil for some 10 minutes.

ANTS

Ants, and many other insects, will avoid any area that's been wiped down with a solution made of equal parts of water and vinegar.

BLEACHING

Forget all your harsh washing treatments for white garments and bedlinen that have become discoloured. The sun provides a totally safe, utterly effective, and, of course, totally free alternative. To bleach by its rays, wash, rinse, and wring the items fairly dry, then spread them on the lawn on a sunny day. If the sun is really fierce, sprinkle some water now and then on the items as they dry. Incidentally, if you have used bleach and find its smell lingers on your fingers, you'll quickly get rid of that unpleasant odour by rinsing your hands with a little vinegar or lemon juice.

BLOOD STAINS

To shift these, soak the affected material in cold salty water for about an hour, and then rinse well with warm soapy water.

BOOKS

Notorious collectors of dust and other small debris, books can be helped to retain their as-new appearance by being taken off the shelves once a year when you should blow off the dust first, then give them a once-over with a feather brush, Finally, before replacing the books on the shelf, open them a few times and close them with a reasonably vigorous slamming action.

BOTTLE CLEANSER

Sediment stains inside of bottles, jars and vases made of glass will clean easily if you half fill the container with white vinegar and shake well. Leave to stand for a few minutes, and then wash or rinse the usual way.

BRASS AND COPPER

Brass objects that appear to have accumulated the dirt of centuries will come up looking like new if they're coated with a mixture composed of equal parts of salt, vinegar and flour, which is washed off after a day or so.

BRONZE

A hard water-resistant alloy, usually consisting of copper and smaller proportions of tin and sometimes zinc and lead, bronze will usually only need dusting with a brush. However, you can considerably brighten bronze ornaments that are beginning to look tarnished by rubbing them now and then with a soft cloth that has been sprinkled with a small amount of almond or olive oil, which is then removed with a soft duster.

BROOMS AND HOUSEHOLD BRUSHES

If you want your brooms and brushes to sweep clean, they, of course, have to be clean themselves in the first place or else you'll just be spreading further dirt around. Soft brooms and brushes will clean up a treat by washing them in warm soapy water to which 1 teaspoon of sodium bicarbonate has been added, and then rinsing them thoroughly in clean water. Treat hard brooms and brushes the same way, but add 1 dessertspoon of salt per pint of water to the final rinse. Extra tip: to ensure that broom bristles retain their shape, always store them head upward.

BRUSHES, PAINT

A painting brush that's encrusted with dried-out paint can usually be given a new lease of life by boiling it in undiluted vinegar, leaving it to stand for a couple of hours and then washing it in hot, soapy water.

BURNT SAUCEPANS

If you've badly burnt the inside of a pot or pan, you may be able to salvage it for future use by covering the affected area with a solution made of equal parts of water and vinegar and bringing this to the boil, then remove from the heat and let stand overnight.

CARPETS, RESTORING COLOUR

You can often at least somewhat enhance the colours of carpet that has faded by rubbing the area that has become discoloured with a cloth impregnated with a mixture of 3 parts of boiling water to 1 part of vinegar.

CARPETS, DEODORISING

Carpets are very good at absorbing small molecules of matter and then gradually releasing them back into the air. In other words, they're great traps that over time accumulate traces of all kinds of unpleasant odours. Fortunately, you can deodorise your carpet cheaply and effectively by sprinkling some sodium bicarbonate on it 10 minutes or so before you run the vacuum cleaner over it.

CARPETS, GETTING RID OF A DENT

If there are deep dents in your carpet caused by the feet of heavy furniture, the depressed pile can be made to rise again by placing an ice cube on it and leaving it for a few hours. When the ice has melted, place a couple of layers of clean white cloth over the affected area and press with an iron set at moderate heat.

CARPET SHAMPOO

Clean carpets with a soft brush dipped in a solution of 1 gallon of water and 1 cup of vinegar. Note that you should always first test this method on an inconspicuous area of the carpet in case its colours are not fast.

CHEWING GUM

This will usually dissolve, even when old and hardened on fabrics like carpets, clothes and upholstery, by the application of hot vinegar. Alternatively, apply ice to the gum until it freezes and you will then usually find it easy to lift away from the area.

CHOCOLATE STAINS

Soak in club soda, white clothing that has become marked by chocolate, be it by drink or melted bar, before washing as usual.

CHROMIUM

Items electroplated with chromium, either to increase hardness or resistance to corrosion, will clean up a treat with a white cloth soaked in vinegar and then polished.

COCONUT MATTING

To restore coconut matting, wash it first in quite hot soapy water, then rinse well in cooler water to which some salt has been added.

COOKING SMELLS

Eliminate these from your kitchen by boiling a cup of water to which you've added a tablespoon of vinegar.

COPPER

To restore the original bright finish to copper surfaces, wipe them vigorously with a paper towel, dampened, not soaked, with a solution of equal parts of lemon juice and vinegar. Finish by polishing with a soft, dry clean white cloth.

COTTON

White cotton materials that somehow your washing machine fails to deal with satisfactorily, may regain their original whiteness, by being placed into a solution of nearly boiling water to which 1 teaspoon of sodium bicarbonate per gallon has been added as well as some soap to make a lather. Boil for 15 minutes or so before rinsing items well in cold water.

CRAYON MARKS

If your child's artistic endeavours have left crayon marks on the wall or wallpaper, these can usually be shifted by rubbing them gently with a dampened sponge that's been sprinkled with a pinch or two of sodium bicarbonate.

CRYSTAL

Adding a tablespoon of vinegar to the final rinse when washing crystal glassware will impart an extra sparkle.

CURTAIN RINGS AND FITMENTS

Curtain rings, runners and other fitments that have yellowed or become grimy, will clean up beautifully if you let them soak for a couple of hours in a bowl filled with a solution of 2 parts of water to 1 of vinegar, then rubbing them dry with rough towelling. Incidentally, applying a trace of beeswax or silicone furniture polish to curtain rods will make runners move freely.

CUTLERY – BONE HANDLES

Stains on cutlery handles made of bone will usually respond well to being rubbed with a dampened white cloth that was dipped in salt. The same method can be used for most composition handles, but do always test it first on an inconspicuous area in case the composition material happens to be one that reacts badly to concentrated salt.

DRAINS, TO CLEAN AND UNBLOCK

To clear the odour from a smelly drain – or to clear it when it's not too blocked with grease or other debris – mix 8 fluid ounces of vinegar with 3 ounces of sodium bicarbonate and pour the solution into the drain. Leave for a quarter of an hour or so, and then run hot water down the drain to finish the job.

EGG

If you're unfortunate enough to drop a raw egg on your carpet, you'll find it a lot easier to clean if you cover it first with salt, as this will bind it, so making it more straightforward to remove the mess.

ENAMELWARE

Although no longer as popular as it once was, enamelware is still preferred by many cooks. While food that has stuck to enamelware can be removed by soaking the utensils in hot water and scrubbing them with a brush, stains will often remain. However, gentle rubbing with a clean cloth sprinkled with vinegar and a little salt will soon get rid of these.

FRUIT STAINS

To remove fruit stains from white fabric, such as a tablecloth that suffered a mishap during dinner, repeatedly dip the item in boiling water. If that doesn't work, dabbing the affected area with lemon juice will almost certainly bring success.

FURNITURE, HEAT MARKS

In most cases, the marks left behind by hot dishes having been placed on polished tables can be removed – or at least made less apparent – by rubbing the marks with a mixture of turpentine and linseed oil, which is prepared by heating ½ pint of the oil for 10 minutes and, when this has cooled down, adding ½ pint of turpentine.

FURNITURE, SCRATCHES

To considerably conceal, even possibly, virtually eliminate, scratches in solid wooden furniture, apply a small amount of cod liver oil to them. Leave for a day or so before applying new polish.

GILT PICTURE AND MIRROR FRAMES

Gilt frames – and other gilded objects – can be cleaned by gently using a clean cloth that is impregnated with warm turpentine. However, do not use this method if the gilt is peeling or showing cracks in it.

GREASY PANS

Wipe the inside of greasy pans and frying pans with newspaper before washing them, either by hand or in the dishwasher.

This serves the dual aims of ensuring that they come out cleaner from the wash and that less grease goes down the drains where it may eventually clog them.

GREASE ON CARPETS

If you've dropped some greasy food on your carpet, remove as much of the food as you can, then heavily sprinkle the affected area with sodium bicarbonate and rub this in well with a clean cloth. Leave the sodium bicarbonate for a couple of hours so it can absorb the grease from the carpet fibre and then vacuum clean.

INK STAINS

After soaking the stained fabric in milk for an hour, smear the stain with a paste composed of vinegar and flour mixed to the consistency of toothpaste. Once the paste has fully dried, wash the fabric as normal.

IVORY

Ivory ornaments can be easily cleaned with a paste made of whiting powder – white chalk that has been ground and washed – and lemon juice. Coat the item with the paste, leave it to dry, and polish with furniture cream. See separate entry for Piano Keys.

KETTLE DESCALER

After covering the element with equal quantities of water and vinegar, bring it to the boil and leave to stand overnight. Next morning, brush off the loosened sediment and rinse thoroughly.

LEATHER FURNITURE

Leather furniture covering that's seen better days can be re-juvenated with a soft white cloth dampened with a mixture of 2 parts of linseed oil and 1 part of vinegar. Be sure to shake the mixture thoroughly in a screw-top bottle or jar before applying.

LINEN

To stop linen from becoming discoloured while in lengthy storage, wrap it in dark paper.

LINOLEUM

Bring back the as-new shine to kitchen or bathroom lino flooring by washing it with a mixture of half a cup of white vinegar added to 1 gallon of warm water.

MARBLE

While soap and water will clean marble, stubborn marks may occasionally remain. Briefly rub these marks with a clean white cloth that has been liberally sprinkled with lemon juice or vinegar, but make sure to rinse away any traces of these acids or they may create marks of their own. If the marks are very hard to shift, leave the lemon juice or vinegar on the surface for a few minutes before rinsing thoroughly.

MICROWAVE OVEN ODOURS

At times the smell of certain foods, such as fish, just lingers and lingers in the microwave after you've cooked them, but heating a cup of water to which you've added a quarter cup of vinegar in the oven will soon banish the unwelcome odour.

MILDEW

A coating or discoloration caused by various saprotrophic fungi that develop in a damp atmosphere on the surface of stored food, fabrics, wallpaper, and so on, mildew can occasionally be incredibly difficult to remove. However, it can usually be cleared by either soaking the affected item in white vinegar or by dabbing it with lemon juice and then putting it out in bright sunlight for a few hours.

MUD

Mud can be almost impossible to shift once it's been left to set and harden in clothes. However, this should see even the most obstinate mud on its way: soak the affected part of the garment for half an hour or so in a quart of warm water to which you've added 1 tablespoon of white vinegar and 1 teaspoon of detergent, then rinse thoroughly.

OIL PAINTINGS

If these are of any value, you'd be wise not to attempt cleaning these yourself other than by lightly dusting them with a very soft brush. For paintings that aren't that valuable, a very gentle wipe with a white cloth dampened with methylated spirits (that's alcohol which has been denatured) may do the trick.

PAINTING SMELLS

After redecorating a room, you can greatly reduce the smell of fresh paint by placing a saucer of vinegar in it. Alternatively, a couple of slices of a raw Spanish onion will also work – that's if you find the smell of onion less offensive than that of paint.

PAINT REMOVAL

To soften hardened paint splashes that fell on glass while decorating, rub them with hot undiluted vinegar. Then scrape them off and clean the glass as usual.

PATENT LEATHER

Ordinary shoe polish will usually be less than effective with belts and handbags made of patent leather, as the material does not absorb it. Instead, use a small amount of petroleum jelly, also known as petrolatum, which will stop the surface of these items from drying and forming cracks.

PERSPIRATION STAINS

Before washing a garment that's badly stained with dried perspiration, dab the affected area with a little bit of white vinegar, and then wash it as usual.

PET ODOURS

The smell of pet urine can be eradicated by spraying the affected area with a solution of 3 parts water to 1 part of vinegar. By the way, if you want cats to stay away from an area, just sprinkle neat vinegar on it and that will discourage them from going near it.

PEWTER

Pewter is a generic name for any of the various alloys containing mainly tin, some lead and, at times, small amounts of other metals, such as copper and antimony. Although it usually tarnishes slowly, it eventually acquires a dark appearance which can be removed by first rubbing the object vigorously with a mixture of whiting powder and linseed oil, then rubbing away any trace of the mixture before finally polishing with a chamois leather.

PIANO KEYS, IVORY

Keys that have become badly yellowed will usually respond well to being rubbed with a clean white cloth that has been dampened with eau de Cologne. Alternatively, put enough whiting powder into a strong solution of potash (potassium carbonate) to make a thick putty-like paste which is applied to the keys and left for about 12 hours, after which it is removed and the keys are polished with chalk. Note that these methods should not be used on musical instrument keys that are made of something other than ivory, for example, plastic, as is often the case with modern keyboards.

PLAYING CARDS

Ensure that you're running a clean game by removing accumulated finger marks from playing cards that have become grubby by rubbing their surfaces gently with a small ball made from compressed breadcrumbs.

POLISHED SURFACES, SCRATCHES

Scratches or spots on polished surfaces, such as tabletops, will just about disappear if you rub them gently with white vinegar and then polish them before the vinegar dries fully.

QUARRY TILES

Attractive though it can be, quarry tiles flooring does have a tendency to eventually develop white patches that mar the finish, but these will soon vanish if you rub them briskly with a clean cloth dampened with a solution made by adding 1 tablespoon of vinegar to 20 fluid ounces of water. Leave the solution to dry naturally on the tiles and repeat the treatment if necessary.

REFRIGERATOR

To keep your refrigerator free from unpleasant odours, place an opened box of baking soda in it.

RUST MARKS ON FABRIC

Rust marks on white clothing will probably disappear – or at least be reduced considerably – by the application of hot lemon juice, or, if the marks have been there some time, by rubbing them gently with a paste made from lemon juice and salt and then putting the item out in the sun to bleach.

Rust, on Metal

Household goods made from iron or steel, with the exception of stainless steel, or which are 'tinned' (steel or iron with a thin covering of tin), are almost certainly bound to show signs of rust eventually as a reddish-brown oxide coating forms on the underlying material because of the combined action of oxygen and moisture. This action will be delayed if lard is rubbed on items that come into contact with food and lanolin applied to other metal goods, such as tools. Existing rust, if not too deep, can usually be removed with a rag that's been dipped in paraffin.

Scorch Marks

If you're unlucky enough to scorch something while ironing, immediately soak the affected area in cold milk. The chances are that the scorch mark will disappear, or at least be minimised. Alternatively, lightly rub the scorch mark with a lint-free cloth soaked in vinegar. If that still doesn't succeed, try rubbing it gently with a silver coin.

Scorched Iron Sole

Dark or burned stains on the sole of an iron will usually be removed by rubbing them with a warm solution of equal parts of vinegar and salt.

Shoes

Run out of shoe polish? Rub them with the inside of a banana peel, and then buff them with a soft cloth for a super shine.

Shower Head

If your shower has become a trickle because of accumulated limescale, you can restore its full flow by dismantling it and soaking the pieces in a bowl of white vinegar for a couple of hours. Clean off any remaining sediment with a stiff brush and rinse the parts before reassembling them.

SILVER

An extremely effective and inexpensive alternative to proprietary silver cleaners can be made by dissolving fine whiting powder in methylated spirits. Gently rub the solution on the silver with a clean cloth, using a toothbrush to get into any awkward corners. When the solution is nearly dry, rub it off with a leather. More severely tarnished silver can be cleaned by immersing it for a few minutes in an aluminium saucepan filled with water to which ½ ounce of sodium bicarbonate per pint has been added, then rinsing the items well and drying them. This method will also work with silver plate. By the way, don't delay emptying the saucepan or the mixture may damage its finish.

SPONGES

As they're used for cleaning, sponges tend to accumulate dirt themselves. To restore a natural sponge to its original condition, rinse out any trapped soap and soak it for a couple of hours in a quart of water to which you've added 2 tablespoons of vinegar or lemon juice. Sponges made from artificial material – rubber, plastic, and so on – will clean up a treat by soaking them for half an hour or so in a solution of 2 ounces of sodium bicarbonate to 1 pint of warm water, and then rinsing them thoroughly in cold water.

STAINLESS STEEL

Although by definition, this material – a type of steel resistant to corrosion as a result of the presence of large amounts of chromium and used in cutlery, cookware and sinks – is supposed to remain stain free, some marks may appear after prolonged use, but the gentle application of whiting powder will soon remove them. Alternatively, use a pinch or two of sodium bicarbonate dissolved in a little bit of water.

TARNISHING

Metal objects tarnish, that is lose their natural shine, because of exposure to air or moisture resulting in surface oxidation and discoloration. When storing such objects for any length of time, you can prevent tarnishing by giving them a light coating of petroleum jelly or lanolin.

TEAPOTS

Tannin, which is present in tea, will over a period of time mark the inside of teapots with stubborn staining. This will, however, easily disappear if you fill the teapot with a solution of warm water and sodium bicarbonate (the quantities are not critical, but a teaspoon of sodium bicarbonate is about right for an average-size teapot), leave it to stand for an hour, and then rinse very thoroughly to get rid of all traces of the sodium bicarbonate.

TEA AND COFFEE STAINS ON GLASS AND CHINA

Soak the stained items in hot vinegar for a quarter of an hour or so, and then wash thoroughly in the usual way. If the stains are really hard to shift, add a small amount of salt to the vinegar and rub on the stains with a clean white cloth.

TAR AND BITUMEN MARKS

Tar or bitumen on upholstery or carpets can be very difficult to remove, but may respond satisfactorily by first covering the affected area with lard or margarine, then washing it in lukewarm water, and finally washing it in hot soapy water.

UPHOLSTERY CLEANER

When there's a stain or mark on upholstery and you've no suitable cleaner at hand, try a small amount of ordinary shaving cream as an interim measure.

VASES

The inside of transparent vases all too quickly can become discoloured and even somewhat opaque. The easy way to clean them is to put a little vinegar and some sand in them, then shake them several times so that the vinegar impregnated sand scours the inside. Of course, ensure that the open top of the vase is sealed with some cling film held into place with a rubber band so that the liquid doesn't splash all over the place when the vase is shaken.

WATER STAINS

Polished wood surfaces that have suffered water stains can usually be treated successfully by gently rubbing in a mixture of cigarette ash and castor oil.

WINDOWS

What works best for cleaning windows will depend on the type of dirt that has accumulated on them. For windows streaked with traces of soil and/or grease, an alkali – that's a soluble mineral salt, such as baking soda or washing soda mixed with warm water – will perform best. If the windows are marred by hard water deposits you'll be better served by using a mixture of about a quart of lukewarm water to which you've added a couple of tablespoons of vinegar. To make windows really sparkle after cleaning, go over them with a clean blackboard eraser. By the way, forget buying expensive chamois leather for cleaning windows or other glass, such as mirrors or tabletops – scrunched-up old newspapers dampened with vinegar will do the job just as well.

WINE STAINS

These can be very difficult to eradicate, especially if they've been left to set, but will usually respond favourably to being rubbed with a mixture of salt and lemon juice and then being washed with warm water and soap. Fresh wine stains will usually disappear without a trace if squirted almost immediately with a soda siphon.

WOODEN KITCHEN UTENSILS

Stains on these will usually disappear by scrubbing with salt water, making sure to move the brush along the grain. Greasy stains will respond to being scrubbed in the same way with hot water with an added pinch of sodium bicarbonate.

ZINC

This is really quite a soft material and will mark easily if cleaned with harsh abrasives, so wash zinc with a solution of warm water and sodium bicarbonate.

SEND US YOUR FAVOURITE RECIPE FOR A CHANCE TO

WIN £500!

The publishers of *The Nostalgic Cook Book* hope
that you've enjoyed the many and varied recipes that appear
in this book.

If you have a favourite recipe that you'd like to be featured in our
next cook book, please send it to us and, if it's used, you will
automatically be entered in our

GRAND DRAW WITH A FIRST PRIZE OF £500!

❧

Entering the competition couldn't be simpler. Just write out your
recipe and send it together with your name, address, and phone
number to us either by post to Favourite Recipes, Emery House,
Greatbridge Road, Romsey, SO51 0AD or by email to
info@nostalgicrecipes.co.uk

What's more, you can increase your chances of being our lucky
Grand Prize winner by submitting as many entries as you wish.

❧

PLEASE NOTE: Every recipe submitted should include a list of the
ingredients and their quantities as well as a short description of the
'method' used to prepare, cook and serve the dish, as well as an
indication of the number of people it will serve. Please also add a short
note about anything pertinent or interesting about the recipe – such as it
having being handed down many generations in your family, or being a
regional specialty, or, for example, having been created by you because
you liked the particular combination of flavours involved.

Index